No Longer Little

No Longer Little

parenting tweens with grace and hope

Hal & Melanie Young

GREAT WATERS PRESS
MAKING BIBLICAL FAMILY LIFE PRACTICAL

No Longer Little

Advance printing, May 2018. Printed and bound in the United States of America.

Publisher's Cataloging-in-Publication Data

Names: Young, Hal, author |Young, Melanie, author.
Title: No longer little : parenting tweens with grace and hope / Hal and
    Melanie Young.
Description: Advance printing.| Smithfield, North Carolina: Great Waters
    Press, 2018. | Includes index.
Identifiers: ISBN 978-1-938554-21-6
Subjects: Parenting—Religious aspects—Christianity | Preteens—Religious
    life | Preteens—Family relationships
Classification: LCC BV4529 | DDC 248.845

Contents

Introduction

This was one of those things nobody warned us about.

When our first son was born, we had already been reading about the mental development of boys. They don't get the fine motor skills as early as their sisters, the researchers said, and that means they don't fit in to the traditional school program right away. Take your time, they recommended, and don't push them too hard at the beginning.

So, when he asked his mother to teach him to read early, we were skeptical. And yet he turned out to be a precocious student. By nine years old, he was already way ahead of his age group. *Wow, we thought. Our son is brilliant, and homeschooling is awesome, and we're awesome, too.*

Then the wheels fell off. He couldn't concentrate, he couldn't grasp the next concepts, and math took three hours if we let it. Pride goes before a fall, right?

This same child was prayed over from the womb. We read him the Bible and had him in the grown-up worship service with us from the time he was still in diapers. He memorized the children's catechism and pretended to be John the Baptist and other characters from the Bible.

Then, at age nine, in traffic, he announced from the back of the van, "I think I'm an atheist."

Nobody told us this was coming.

No one warned us that the eight-year-old that we could give five consecutive errands all over the house and he'd never forget a thing would become the eleven-year-old who we'd send to get the car keys and then find wandering all over the house forty-five minutes later, completely clueless.

No one told us that our other sweet boy, the one who was born middle-aged and responsible, would turn into a green rage monster at fourteen. It didn't last long and now he's a middle-aged college student (or at least acts like it), but still...

We had read the books about effective child discipline and early learning and all those things up through elementary school years. We'd been warned to brace ourselves for the teenage challenges to come. But we don't remember anyone telling us that preteens—the middle schoolers—would be especially challenging.

When things started to change in our relationship with our first son, we didn't know what to think. It wasn't until about the third time we went through it, two sons later, that we realized there was a pattern here—that maybe the struggles we'd had with our first and second sons, and then with our third—maybe it wasn't a problem in our parenting or a defect in our children, but part of the normal growing up process. The key, we've learned through parenting eight kids through this stage, is understanding what was happening, when to expect it, and how to navigate through it.

And that's why we wrote this book—to share the lessons we learned and wish we'd known the first time we saw the change.

It Wasn't Just Us, and It's Not Just You

When we wrote our first book, *Raising Real Men*, we realized a large segment of our readership was parents with preteen boys. That seemed to be the age when first-time parents discovered they didn't understand their little boys any more—and as we learned, it was because something was changing, and they didn't know what to do about it.

Everybody knows about the changes of adolescence—the growth spurt, the development of broader shoulders and whiskers, or the transition to a womanly figure. As young people ourselves, we heard about it in health class or gym, or embarrassing conversations with a parent. But those preparatory sessions all pointed at the external changes which couldn't be denied.

What they *didn't* tell us is that all that hormonal activity that teenagers endure actually began long before many external changes appeared. The coach who knew you only as a sixth-grader never saw the change in personality and temperament that happened a year or two earlier. And the fourth-grade teacher who didn't know you in primary school couldn't make a comparison with the student she saw in her classroom.

Before the boy's voice cracks or the girl has her first period, the hormones have been stimulating internal changes for years. This comes out in the emotions, intellect, behavior, and spiritual life long before the first growth spurt. And that's what gives parents fits.

It's a Crucial Time

The importance of the preteen years is often underestimated. This is particularly true in the spiritual life. In separate studies completed in the early 2000's, researchers found that children who left the faith of their parents, the faith they'd been raised in, had begun to experience doubts when they entered the preteen years.[1] Carol Barnier, a pastor's daughter who completely abandoned

---

[1] Brian D. Ray, *Gen2 Survey: A spiritual and educational survey on Christian millennials* (2015); Ken Ham *et al*, *Already Gone* (2009)

Christianity for a time before coming to faith in her adult years, said that she first questioned the truth of the Bible and the existence of God as a middle-schooler—but swallowed her questions for fear of her parents' reaction. That's a fearsome thought to a Christian parent.

But it's not just the relationship with God which is disturbed. Often, the relationship with parents can be strained, or even broken, during these years. We believe the many of the difficulties parents experience with their 16—and 17-year-olds may have had their start when the child was 11 or 12.

So, this book will talk a great deal about relationships. We'll share practical ideas about managing school, emotions, and all that, because it helps to have techniques to regain some organization in a very confusing and rapidly changing time. But ultimately, we think, the key to understanding and making it through this period hinges on relationships and principles, more than rules and checklists.

There's Hope

We are very glad to be able to say that our nine-year-old prospective atheist grew into a mature Christian man who made a significant impact for Christ on two college campuses and has a leadership role in his church today. The distracted middle-schooler who took forever to finish his arithmetic went on to complete calculus in high school and earn a degree in economics in college. There is hope for you and your preteen, even when it seems hard to believe.

We'd like to share some of what we learned as we walked through this transition with seven of our children—as we watch the opening changes with our eighth.

Getting Bigger 1

With eight children to manage and a fair drive to our church, Sunday morning has always been a bustle in our house. Older kids are expected to manage their own preparation so we parents can focus on helping the younger kids. That means of course that sometimes one of the kids had to get dressed twice. To be fair, since our first six children were boys, there were lots of similar clothes in nearly-but-not-quite the same sizes; sometimes they could trade around, sometimes not.

Often Melanie would look up from brushing somebody's hair or changing a diaper and observe, "Son! Those pants are too short for you—where are the khakis you wore last week?"

"Mom," he would reply, slightly pained, "these *are* the ones I wore last week. And my shoes are too tight now."

Frequently, that was true. When our boys hit their growth spurts, they would grow so fast sometimes you could almost see it while you watched. The same son would return to the room he just left, looking visibly taller. Of *course*, last week's khakis were too short.

Puberty is the process of physical change in the transition from childhood to adulthood, reaching sexual maturity at the end. When we think of this time, we probably think about cracking voices and training bras. In fact, the onset of puberty is often counted from the time a boy's voice first breaks.

However, the physical changes that are about to occur are *massive*. Just consider the end points of the transition, from a slightly chubby

7- or 8-year-old, to an angular young man learning to shave or a shapely young woman learning to carry herself with grace. At the start, they're clearly children; at the end, they could become parents themselves. It's a huge transition, it takes years to complete, and the starting phase is earlier and longer than most of us expect—and it affects a lot more than external appearance.

Where has our little boy gone?

"My son seems like a different person lately," a mother asks at a conference. "He's gotten so moody and irritable. I wonder where my sweet little boy went... what went wrong?"

When we mention he's probably beginning the changes of puberty, she argues, "I don't think so. He's still just a little boy!"

That's a common reaction, just like the feeling "They're growing up so fast!" It's true, they are, and it's even faster than you thought. The hormones that will change him from a boy to a man start flowing many months before you start to see the physical changes. Those changes become evident as much as two years after the hormonal shift begins.

Scientists haven't been able to pin down what it is exactly that causes the process of puberty to start, beyond the central role of hormones to begin the physical development. One thing we didn't expect ourselves was the emotional changes which suddenly appeared in our sons. Frankly, they got—well, *hormonal*—moody, irritable, unpredictable in their personalities. If they'd been girls, we'd have recognized this immediately, but nobody warned us that boys get the same symptoms. Wow, do they ever. We called it PMS, for "pre-manhood syndrome," in our houseful of boys.

This should not be a surprise for parents of either sons *or* daughters. Researchers have found both sexes have hormonal surges exceeding *fifty times* the normal, stable levels they have in adulthood. It's no wonder their behavior seems extreme—we parents wouldn't handle that sort of tsunami very well ourselves, even when we understand what's happening!

What's coming soon

We'll deal with the emotional aspects of puberty and adolescence in the next chapter. They rush to the forefront because the earliest physical changes can be easily overlooked—and are often concealed by the embarrassed young person.

Understanding and explaining what's happening is further complicated by the normal variation in human development. We had six sons, and five of them played football in a community league. The youngest players, in the "Mighty Mite" division, were all as short as their shoulder pads were wide. The junior varsity and varsity players had more variation in their size, but what you'd expect to see—tackles and guards aren't built like QBs and running backs, after all. But oh, the youth division—what a spectrum of sizes and stages of development! These guys were all middle schoolers, but every shape a boy could take; some were probably sprouting their first whiskers, while others were still softly padded with "baby fat." All of it was in the perfectly normal range of time and pace for puberty's onset.

We saw similar things in our friends' families where girls were concerned. One family's daughters developed early and always seems two or three years ahead of their actual age in their appearance and the way they carried themselves. Other families' girls lagged behind, and always seemed more comfortable playing with friends a year or two younger than themselves. Perfectly normal.

What to expect in your daughter

Generally, girls start this transition earlier than boys—usually about two years sooner. There is some controversy how to mark the very starting point of puberty in girls. One traditional sign is the development of breast buds, yet while girls seem to be starting this development earlier than they used to, other changes of puberty such as brain changes are not following suit. Some doctors believe this is due to estrogens in the environment and should not be considered the true onset of puberty.[1]

One of the first things parents of girls notice is a need for more deodorant. When puberty gets underway, the changes in a girl's internal chemistry will change her body odor, she'll likely develop a more oily complexion (hello, acne), and she'll need to start washing her hair more often. Privately, she'll also start to grow pubic hair, very sparsely at first, and a couple of years later, hair in her armpits and later darker hair on her legs. We can help our girls by keeping an eye out for these changes and reminding them to take showers, use deodorant, and eventually teaching them to shave their armpits or legs, if women do that in your culture. During this time, her body fat will begin to redistribute, too. She'll begin to get a curvier figure as her waist thins out while her hips and breasts become more woman-like. As her breasts begin to develop, it can help both the tenderness and the embarrassment to get her a soft sports bra to provide a little protection and coverage. Don't put this off, thinking, "I can't believe I'm buying a bra for my eight year old (or whatever age)." It's better to be a little early with this than to be too late and leave her feeling awkward about her body or even subjected to teasing. Other kids can be incredibly cruel to girls who develop sooner than others, sometimes even questioning their

[1] Elizabeth Weil, "Puberty Before Age 10: A New 'Normal'?" *The New York Times Magazine*, 30 Mar 2012

virtue. As ridiculous as that is, if this is your daughter, she will need a lot of reassurance and encouragement.

Her growth rate will accelerate, too. It can happen unbelievably fast; it's a little unsettling to be thinking of your daughter as a little girl and suddenly realize she's almost as tall as her mother. Because girls typically start this phase before the boys their age, it can make them feel awkward and uncertain themselves, as they might pass the boys their age in height for a time. Women in our family tend to be tall; Melanie remembers looking around and wondering whether there would be any boys tall enough for her, and Hal's mother had the same experience when she was growing up. Both of them were relieved to see Hal was nine inches taller than his fiancée Melanie!

Girls need a lot of positive reinforcement when they are feeling so strange about their own bodies. Don't hesitate to tell your daughter she's beautiful. We live in a time when it's impossible to avoid images (and idols) of women who are impossibly thin and shapely—impossible in a very literal sense: many advertising photos are digitally altered to a standard that no real woman could ever attain.

Some parents worry that telling their daughters they are attractive will make them proud or vain. When we search the Scriptures, though, we see many women described as lovely or beautiful by those that love them. We don't want our daughters to worry that they'll never meet some fantasy standard of perfect beauty; we need to point out how God has made each of them lovely to *His* standard, not the glamour-merchants'.

A girl's first menstrual cycle is referred to as *menarche*, which comes from the Greek words meaning "beginning month." Most girls have begun their cycles by 15 or 16, but it can begin as early as 8 years old. That means we need to be talking about this part of our daughter's biology and upcoming changes very early indeed!

We explain this process to our girls as their bodies preparing for the time when they'll marry and become mothers. At the start of each monthly cycle, the hormone estrogen causes the woman's uterus to build up a soft lining which could receive and nurture a developing baby. About halfway through the month, the lining is complete and the ovaries will release an egg which travels down the fallopian tubes to the uterus or womb.

If the woman has had sexual intercourse with her husband during this time, the sperm will be swimming up the uterus and fallopian tubes in the opposite direction. If the sperm and egg meet and combine, a baby is conceived, and the newly fertilized egg will implant in that soft uterine lining. There it will grow and develop until the time for birth.

The last half of the cycle, the woman's hormone balance changes to supply progesterone, a different hormone which will maintain the uterine lining to protect the developing baby—whether or not an egg actually implanted! At the end of the cycle, if conception actually occurred, the baby itself is sending hormonal signals back to the mother's body, and the high progesterone level will continue throughout the pregnancy.

But if there's no baby in the womb at the end of the cycle, the woman's body will shift back to producing estrogen, and since the uterine lining is no longer needed, it will loosen and pass out of her body as blood and tissue. This is referred to as menstrual flow, or colloquially as a period, and when it's completed in a few days, the cycle begins again.

It's good to explain that the last week of the month, with hormones changing and some significant things happening inside, many women feel more emotional than usual (both irritable and sad) and may feel some soreness or cramping as that lining comes off. This is normal and there are things that can help both moodiness and discomfort (some as simple as getting additional calcium)—and we need to be sure we've prepared our daughters for this unfamiliar experience and help them through it!

Part of that support is encouraging her that menstruation is private, but nothing to be ashamed of. It's part of the process God created to bring new life into our world, and any discomfort or unpleasantness involved is a result of Adam and Eve's rebellion—and a reminder of our need of a Redeemer!

We believe that in celebrating what it means to be a woman, and the incredible gift that God has given our daughters to be the carriers of new life, our girls will be more likely to have the right attitude about themselves.

What to expect in your son

If the preteen girls feel self-conscious about their height, it's just as true for the boys. Our sons generally start puberty a year or two later than girls, but the range is still quite wide. The physical changes usually start between 9 and 15 years old, and the early signs of physical change are not as obvious.[2]

For all their noise and boldness in other areas, boys can become surprisingly modest about their bodies at this age. The first external changes are enlargement of the testes and scrotum and the start of pubic hair—not something parents are likely to observe! What's more obvious is the emotional turmoil prompted by their hormonal surge.

The chemical changes underway are often signaled by a downright *stench* around your boys. In the movie *Amazing Grace,* William's

---

[2] Sarah-Jayne Blakemore, Stephanie Burnett, and Ronald E. Dahl. "The Role of Puberty in the Developing Adolescent Brain." *Human Brain Mapping* 31.6 (2010): 926-33. *PubMed Central.* Web. 10 Aug. 2015.

friends encourage him toward marriage with the warning that bachelors "die alone in rooms that smell of feet and armpits."[3] We can attest to this environment in a home with six boys—at least two of them going through this transition at any point in a ten year period. He'll need more showers than he ever thought possible, stronger shampoo, a new expectation of deodorant, and a reminder to change clothes regularly. Acne may be an afterthought to parents but a major concern for the boy.

The young man's growth spurt may be an awkward time simply because his limbs are rapidly becoming longer than he realized, and he may become accident prone for a season. At the same time, though, the accelerated gain in height may come as a relief. A younger brother may feel left behind as his older siblings—brothers or sisters—gain their stature years before he does. As a practical matter, it may be good practice to avoid spending too much on clothes or shoes while your preteen is in growth mode; ours went through several sizes in a year, so it made sense to either keep the wardrobe to an easily-replaced minimum, or plan a path for quick hand-me-downs.

While girls who develop early seem to suffer more socially, with boys it's the late developers who struggle. If your son still looks like a little boy when his friends are becoming broader and more muscular, you'll need to encourage him to be patient and not discouraged. His voice will change and his height will climb at the right time for him.

One of the normal changes of puberty can be truly alarming to guys. In the months just prior to their growth spurt, boys will often gain some weight, and more than half of boys will see some puffiness or enlargement around their breast area. This is normal and harmless, and it usually flattens out as they get older. Still, you might want to be understanding if he seems unwilling to go shirtless for a time— even when swimming.

[3] *Amazing Grace.* Directed by Michael Apted. (Los Angeles: Walden Media, 2006)

At some point in this process, his voice will begin to change. Like many things in life, the end result is desirable—most boys probably look forward to having a deeper, manly voice—but the intermediate stages are terrible. Hal was in a children's choir at church as a third and fourth-grader, and he tried his best to sing a lower octave than the rest of his friends—no boy soprano parts for him, thank you!

But when the change begins, the boy's normal pitch seems to drop from the childish treble to exactly their mother's voice... not Dad's admirable bass.

This is mortifying when he picks up the phone thinking a friend is calling, and instead, not only hears the friend's mother, but gets mistaken for his own mom:

"Hey, Molly! How are you doing, girl? I called to see if you wanted to go get a pedicure with me tomorrow!"

Ugh, thinks the young man.

He will probably appreciate it if you don't make too many jokes about his involuntary warbling. It's comforting to be reminded, "You know what? Your voice is getting deeper every day. Before long, people will think you are your dad!" Knowing it's just a phase that pass soon enough makes it easier to bear for now.

Another outward sign of manliness—one that can be shown off and bragged about—is the darkening hair on his chest, arms, and legs. Boys aren't always amused by the patchiness of it at first, particularly when the excitement of the first real whiskers begins to wear off. It may be helpful to point out that many men won't be able to grow a decent mustache or beard until their twenties.

Teaching your son to shave can be a good excuse for some father-son bonding time. You might even get him a bag and some basic shaving and grooming supplies of his own; they're inexpensive and unmistakably masculine. Our older teens discovered retro shaving supplies and ordered old-fashioned after-shave like the barber shop uses. Hal still likes to use the after-shave and cologne his father and grandfather used, so don't discount the value of family traditions in this area!

Boys often continue growing into their late teens, and sometimes even early twenties. Even if their height plateaus, typically their shoulders will continue to broaden and they become much more muscular. Their last growth spurt may come well into their college career or their first job after high school. This is a happy time for a young man!

Physically awkward, but that's not the half of it!

Both boys and girls usually experience awkwardness during puberty. Some of it is the ungainliness of rapidly growing arms and legs. Some of it is from the timing of the secondary sexual characteristics like breasts or beards—whether they appear "too early" or "too late." Sometimes it's the additional weight coming before the growth spurt. The list goes on and on...

But the physical part is really the easiest part for most families. Those huge surges of hormones have lots of other effects, too. Preteens in the throes of early puberty have mood swings, intellectual changes, spiritual doubts, and struggles of different kinds. It's a hard age to get through, especially since the foundations are being laid for the teen and adult years. So, let's dive right in to the stormy waters of preteen emotions and see how to handle the rocks and waves ahead!

The Rollercoaster 2

I t happened one morning in the middle of a family meeting.

We have a large family and as our older kids became more independent, and as we moved from 9-to-5 corporation life to ministry and self-employment, we realized we needed to get the whole family coordinated and reading from the same page. We like to have the whole family's input and buy-in on schedules and activities. Naturally, then, we have lots of family meetings.

And on this morning, in the middle of some piece of mundane business, our 13-year-old suddenly started tearing his hair like a cartoon character. "I can't stand all the *anger* in here!" he shouted.

Startled, the rest of the family looked around the room, question marks floating all about.

"Uh, Son?" one of us finally spoke up. "There's nobody angry but you."

He glanced around, saw the wide-eyed query on all his siblings' faces, then he blushed and shrank back in his seat.

"Oh," he mumbled.

What's going on here?

F or a young boy to change into a man, or a girl into a woman, there are tremendous physical changes and transformations that have to occur. These are started and regulated by the increasing level of hormones in the early-puberty child.

Most parents will have some recent experience with hormones for themselves—like the infamous Pre-Menstrual Syndrome. When the woman's monthly cycle changes her hormonal balance at the end of the month, the result is often emotional—irritability, crankiness, sadness, and malaise. People laugh about it, but the feelings are real, as any woman can tell you.[1]

In the early days of puberty, our children are going through the same things. In fact, we said that our boys were going through PMS—Pre-Manhood Syndrome (it just lasts a couple of years instead of a few days).

The elevated level of hormones necessary to bring about huge and rapid physical change is going to have an emotional impact as well. This is one of the most challenging aspects of parenting this age— the emotional upheaval. The young person's moods are all over the map, and it's like they've climbed on an emotional roller coaster and invited you to join them.

Parents: Do not get on this ride.

In fact, one of the key recommendations we make to parents of preteens is to avoid this thrill ride. If you want to preserve your relationship with your child, you will need to keep your own feet (and heart and mind) on solid ground, in order to give them a point of stability they can cling to. It won't be easy; our kids have a special kind of crazy going on in their heads and hearts, and because they're so close to us, they can truly zero in on behaviors and words that will have the greatest bite.

---

[1] We do not recommend you ask her in the midst of it, or you may suffer from her hormones yourself.

Here be dragons!

n the old days, cartographers often signaled that unknown and probably dangerous things might be found at the margins of their experience. An ancient globe was curiously labeled with the warning *Hic Sunt Dracones!* Here Be Dragons! Roman and Medieval mapmakers would flag unexplored territory "Lions abound," and the Irish satirist Jonathan Swift mused that *"geographers, in Afric maps, / With savage pictures fill their gaps, / And o'er unhabitable downs / Place elephants for want of towns."*[2]

Navigators were on notice: whether it be dragons, lions, or stampeding pachyderms, the incautious traveler should beware.

You've now entered that territory for the parent and the preteen alike.

Strange conversations ensue:

Parent: "Hey, Son—That shirt's dirty. You need to change before you leave."

Reasonable Person: "Oh—I hadn't noticed. I'll go take care of it."

Actual Son's Response: "What do you mean it's dirty? It looks fine to me! You're just too picky. You never like anything I do anyway. You're always getting on my case! You never treat my brother like that. I might as well stay home. I can't do anything to please you!" [exit, in huff]

The parent looking on wonders, "What was *that*?"

That, at least, was what we saw with our sons. Boys tend to respond to their hormonal rush with anger and aggression. It was like living in a house with a pet porcupine. One that has burst into flame. A flaming porcupine.

---

[2] Jonathan Swift, "On Poetry: A Rhapsody" (1733)

Girls may respond to their hormone surge with a different reaction. Melanie walked into the living room recently to find our daughter sobbing on the couch, all alone.

"Honey, what's the matter?" Melanie said, rushing to her side. "Are you okay? Why are you crying?"

"I don't *knooooooooooowww!*" she wailed.

"Then I do," Melanie responded. "Let's talk."

This sort of unexplained or unprovoked sadness and weeping are common in girls, anger and rage with boys, but the full range appears in both sexes at different times. Sometimes the switch from one to the other can cause neck injuries in observers, as the boy who is spoiling for a fight and ready to provoke the world, suddenly finds himself with an irritated older brother on his hands, and starts wailing, "Nobody cares about me!"

Exasperating

These irrational outbursts can certainly test our parental patience. They may actually be worse for the children experiencing them, because they usually don't understand why they feel so *bad*. And this creates a more direct test for the parent.

Before this time, whenever your child felt anger or frustration or sadness, it was usually because something had happened to cause it. Somebody spoke harshly to him, or took away something he wanted, or treated him badly somehow. The emotions followed an identifiable cause.

But emotions have a biochemical component that hormones affect, and attacks of moodiness in the preteen may have no other cause but this chemical state. Now, when your boy experiences a surge of testosterone and feels edgy, irritable, and angry, he looks around to find out what's causing it. *Surely* there must be someone or something causing this feeling; that's always been the case before.

Guess who happens to be there? "You! It must be you!" he thinks, and searches around in his heart for some real or imagined slight or offense.

This is pretty upsetting when you're the target of the anger. It may be totally unjustified, and likely catches you by surprise. However, this is a moment when a parent who resists the temptation to react immediately can find an opportunity to connect with the child's heart.

De-fanging a serpent

When our kids are younger, maybe seven—or eight years old, we try and give them a little heads-up for the changing times to come. It's likely a universal experience for all of us—when we were this age, didn't we all have gloomy days when we thought to ourselves, "Nobody likes me. Nobody cares about me. Nobody understands me...."? Even well-loved children with careful parents and affirming homes go through this. It's something we warn our younger kids about, the same as we clue them in that body changes and growth spurts are on the way.

Why? For some of the same reasons, we think, that God lays out prophecies in the Scripture—because the day will come when our kids can look back and say, "Yes, we were told about this, weren't we? Maybe our parents were right after all!"

So when these emotional eruptions occur, and our child is accusing us of rank injustice or unloving harshness or other things which (hopefully) are not true in the slightest sense... instead of reacting to the accusation, we'll listen first.

We find it's helpful to counter this kind of confrontation by saying, "Why don't we sit down here and talk about this? Tell me what's going on. What are you thinking here?" And then really, truly, *listen*—let them talk through it. Ask questions if you need to clarify what's on their mind, but don't respond yet. Give them time to get it all out, if they can.

Here's the critical point—our child has an enemy, the oldest in the Book, and the devil seems to take special advantage of this emotional turmoil to tempt our children away from our care and guidance. He'd love to break the trust of the parent/child bond if he can. When our kids are full of strong emotions they can't understand and can't control, the Tempter's quiet narrative is exactly what we all remember—"No one cares about you. No one understands you. No one's on your side. No one really loves you..."

That persistent temptation makes this stage of parenting one of the most crucial. A strong parent-child relationship is vitally important for the teen years coming up, so what better time to lay a minefield for the high school years than by fracturing the God-given relationship with those in the best position to guide them through? And indeed, we hear again and again how parents and children fell out with each other and dissention and rebellion grew up from the middle school years.

Instead, if the emotional rollercoaster beckons but we refuse to climb aboard, we can focus on preserving the relationship and guiding them through this rough time. There needs to be an adult in this relationship and it isn't going to be them.

When we choose not to respond in anger, but instead we sit down and try to understand them, we pull teeth right out of the Serpent. He says, "Nobody cares. Nobody understands," but there we are, saying, "I care. I want to understand. Let's talk."

Does that mean we ignore the disrespect? Certainly not! Now is not the time, though. Remember that proper discipline is not focused on punishment but on correction and teaching—in other words, discipleship—and that isn't effective when the disciple is too overwrought to receive instruction! Whatever discipline is needed can wait until the anger and uproar subsides.

We've had some interesting and unintentionally amusing conversations in these times. One of our children was talking on and on about some imagined slight, then finally stopped and realized, "I'm not making much sense, am I?" No, he certainly wasn't, but it was much more effective for the truth to dawn and come from his own lips, rather than us scolding him for such foolish talk. We've found in many or most cases, allowing them to talk through their complaint will at least get them back off their emotional ledge, and then they're more receptive to reasonable discussion.

Several things can happen at this point. It's entirely possible that we parents actually did do something to cause offense, and we need to repent. It could be the child is in sin, and we need to take them to the Word of God and deal with the situation on that basis.

Sometimes we need to administer a reality check. Young people this age are by definition lacking experience and knowledge, particularly in "grown up" areas from which they've been excluded. This may be a good time to open that doorway a bit and explain why something came about that caused the child grief.

We know of one family whose son suddenly exploded at his dad, "You don't keep your promises! You lied to me! You're just a liar!"

His father was dumbstruck. What on earth was this boy talking about? The parents had always placed the greatest emphasis on honesty and integrity, so this accusation was a serious affront.

But though it was tempting to respond in immediate anger and instant punishment, the father held back for a moment and asked, "What do you mean? Let's talk about this."

"You said we'd go back to our old church," the son began. "You said we'd get to visit sometimes and you never took us. You're a promise breaker!"

Never mind that it had been seven years since they left that church, his dad thought. The boy was only five years old at the time, and he hadn't mentioned it since, but suddenly today it was a relationship-breaking crisis?

As frustrating as this sort of thing is, in the emotional whirlwind of the preteen, it really may be a crisis to him. It's easy to react to this kind of accusation with some rage and frustration of your own. No one takes well to being abused and maligned, especially by their children (and without warning!)... and doubly so, if the accusation is unwarranted, unfair, or untrue. It's tempting to jump into the fray with a few accusations and "explanations" of our own.

On the other hand, you can see it as a great opportunity. The Bible reminds us that only God sees the heart of a man; we humans can only judge by what we see.[3] If our son or daughter has an offense or grudge against us, don't we want to know about it? Even if it's not fair or makes no sense, it's a blessing to find what's in our kids' hearts. Once we know it, we can address it.

"I'm sorry, Son," his dad replied. "I should have explained the situation to you. Not long after we left that church, there were some leadership changes and most of our old friends left. There was no reason to go back. Will you forgive me for not talking to you about that? I didn't realize you were still thinking about it."

---

[3] 1 Samuel 16:7—"For the LORD does not see as a man sees; for man looks at the outward appearance, but the LORD looks at the heart."

Don't worry about pedestals

Some parenting teachers take the approach that fathers and mothers hold authority from God but only tenuously. The message, whether explicit or implied, is that parents need to stay above the fray in some sort of Olympian detachment. It may diminish the child's respect and awe toward her parents if they ever climb down from their pedestal.

This is some kind of late-Victorian claptrap, at best. The fact is, your children are well aware of your imperfections and shortcomings. If you have sinned against your child, even by accident, then you need to repent and seek their forgiveness.

Instead of lowering yourself in their estimation, what you are actually doing is three-fold. First, you're accepting blame for an offense and seeking to restore the relationship, regardless of whom the offended party might be. Secondly, you're demonstrating to your child how much you value the relationship over your supposed pride. But maybe more than this, you're demonstrating to your son or daughter how a Christian responds to rebuke or criticism—if it's a fair rebuke, he should humble himself, confess what he did, and seek forgiveness. You're modeling a behavior which your young people need to learn—which, incidentally, they'll probably need to practice themselves in the next few minutes!

What if you didn't do anything wrong? What if they aren't making any sense? What if *they're* the ones in sin or they simply don't understand the situation?

Sometimes we just need to give them a lesson in reality or at least some perspective they may have missed. Say your daughter is upset that she has more chores to do than her younger sister. You might need to say, "Sweetheart, I know it feels like you're doing a lot more chores than Elizabeth, but you may not remember that you didn't have many chores when you were her age, either. At that age, you were just learning how to do some of the things you do well now. And when she gets a little older, she'll be doing most the same things you are now, too."

Or maybe there's jealousy in the other direction, toward an older sibling. It's normal and healthy for a preteen to want to stretch his wings and become one of the "big kids" (really, the young adults), but there is the reality that he isn't ready for every freedom and liberty all at once. "Son, I know you'd like to have your own computer like Bobby does, but you have to remember he's three years older than you and taking classes online, too. A few years from now, if you're responsible, you probably have the same privileges he does."

Often, though, they're the ones in sin. Maybe he lost his temper and punched his brother, but thinks it's all his brother's fault because he was provoked. Perhaps she threw her brother's computer bag in the floor in a storm of tears, but she thinks he deserved it because he hurt her feelings.

Even if they weren't in sin for the initial conflict, they've probably been disrespectful or unkind to someone in the argument that followed.[4]

We find the Word of God reaches their hearts way better than our words do.

"Son, I know you were angry at what your brother said, but Proverbs tells us that a man who can't control his temper is like a city whose walls are torn down.[5] When a city has high walls, they can decide whether or not to fight a passing army, but when the walls are torn

---

[4] We often remind our kids, especially as they get a little older, "The First Rule of Holes is: *stop digging.*" Once you're in trouble, it's best not to compound it by lying, losing your temper, or showing disrespect.

[5] Proverbs 25:28, *Whoever has no rule over his own spirit / Is like a city broken down, without walls.*

down, any passing enemy can force them into a fight. When you can't control your temper, other people control you. All they have to do is provoke you a little, and here you are, in trouble. It puts you at other people's mercy. Yes, your brother was out of line to tease you like he did and we'll be dealing with that, but when you lost your temper and hit him, you sinned. You did wrong. *'Vengeance is mine , I will repay.' Says the LORD.*[6] You aren't supposed to avenge yourself—and don't tell me it was self-defense. He's your brother and I was right here in the next room. You weren't in any danger, and you could have called a parent in to deal with the problem."

Repentance is sweet

This is usually the point where we can see repentance. When we do, we can't flame off and say, "Well! Can we get past this now?" Instead, we need to rejoice that they've come to this point—remember, the angels in heaven rejoice when a sinner repents, so we should do so as well.[7] Maybe you didn't plan to spend the last half hour on the emotional rollercoaster, or standing on the platform waiting for the child's train to slow down—but that may actually be the most productive time you spend this day, training your son or daughter's character.

Now's a good time to remember the father of the prodigal son.[8] After the younger son had taken his inheritance early and blown the whole thing on wine, women, and song, he came crawling back home a humbled and degraded man. How did his father respond?

Honestly, it would be tempting to say, "It's about time, and you smell like a pig!"

---

[6] Romans 12:19 and other passages
[7] Luke 15:10—*"Likewise, I say to you, there is joy in the presence of the angels of God over one sinner who repents."*—Jesus
[8] Luke 15:11-32

But that's not what happened— the father ran to meet his son with joy that he was restored to him. The story is meant to teach us about God the Father, but it is a good model for us in our parenting, too. The right response to repentance in our children is joy.

It's important to point our kids to Christ when they repent. They need your forgiveness, and the forgiveness of others they may have hurt in their storm, but they need His much more. At the end of one of these outbursts, when you've talked it all out, there can be a time of openness to the forgiveness of God. Sometimes they feel foolish or wretched. They know better than to say the horrible things they said and they feel awful. What a great time to remind them that Christ died so that our sin could be forgiven and that we could be made new.

Note, however, that there were still consequences for the prodigal son. He'd spent his inheritance and it wasn't coming back. Sometimes there will still be consequences for our children's sin, even after they've repented. The unkind actions or harsh words cause real hurt, and there may be restitution or healing yet to come.

When you finally get through to them, you may need to discipline the disrespect or disobedience or whatever the particular sin is. We'll say, "Son (or Daughter), I am so glad you've repented, but you know, you were really disrespectful, and it was in front of the other children. You know I have to discipline that for their sake and for yours."

To our surprise, one of our young people responded, "You know, Mom, you're right. What are we going to do?" Several times we've seen children apologize publicly to their brothers and sisters for showing disrespect to their parents and lack of love to their siblings. That is a sight to cheer the tired parental heart—a child who started completely out of control, changing to one who is repenting of his sin and willing to accept discipline. It's time-consuming to get there, but it is so worth it.

Brains Turn To Mush 3

When our family is confronted with an idea or a decision, we tend to read and talk and analyze it to death—even if the decision isn't immediately confronting us. We wrestled through our children's education before we even had children to educate. We decided as newlyweds in the 1980s that the newly-emerging idea of homeschooling was just the ticket. We'd both been incredibly bored in school and we were excited by the idea of our kids being able to learn on their own schedule and to chase after knowledge without being limited to what the school had planned. We loved the idea of discipling them ourselves and making sure they had a thoroughly Christian education. We couldn't wait.

When the time came to launch this great project, our first child was thrilled. He was a precocious reader, picked up his math facts quickly, and seemed to enjoy school more and more as he grew. He even loved foreign languages when we introduced them in the third grade.

We were convinced our son was brilliant, homeschooling was great, and really, our parenting and teaching skills were awesome, too. Yes, sir, life was sweet.

Then he turned nine, and the wheels fell off the train.

That year, school fell apart. Math was an all-day ordeal. Often, it seemed, it was the only thing we got done. *Everything* he did took forever, and he was constantly getting distracted. School went from a delight to a nightmare. We didn't know if it was him, or us, or our curriculum, or what.

Until it happened to the next child. And the next child. And the next.

It's not your fault—nor theirs

After we lived through this educational crash the third or fourth time, we discovered that it's not unusual at all. In fact, we should have predicted it from what we learned about human development and even through our own experience.

Hal grew up in public school as an insider of sorts—his mother was a teacher, his grandmother was a teacher, his uncle and aunt were teachers. We heard the quiet comment that fourth grade wasn't really meant to introduce much, if any, new material. In our school system, Grade 4 was mostly time to get everybody caught up.

Another catch-up year was planned a few grades later, just before high school. We've heard similar things in another state. And it's no accident these academic pauses serve as bookends to the pre-teen, middle school years.

We've talked about the hormonal changes in our preteens and the effects those hormones have on their bodies and emotions. Those hormones also affect their brains.

When we made our decision for homeschooling, Melanie enrolled in graduate school because she thought she might need a teaching certificate. After all, Hal was in the Air Force, with no guarantee where he might be assigned next, and some states were still prosecuting homeschoolers at the time.[1] We thought a teaching degree might head off problems one day.

Nearly every course she took her first year started with a discussion of early childhood development. We heard over and over again

---

[1] Thankfully, homeschooling has been legal in all fifty states for quite a while now. If you're interested in knowing more about legal requirements and what's involved in starting your own school, contact the Home School Legal Defense Association (website http://www.hslda.org/)

about Swiss psychologist Jean Piaget and his theories of cognitive development. He identified this time as a transition between the "Concrete Operations" stage, when children can understand and manipulate real numbers and actual situations, and the start of the "Formal Operations" state, when abstract thinking becomes possible.

Classical education theory made the same division centuries earlier, when students were moved from the "Grammar" stage, where they mainly learn and memorize facts about the world around them, to the more analytical "Logic" stage, where they learn how to connect and manipulate those facts. In high school, they would move to the "Rhetoric" stage of learning.

Whatever you call it, it's a time of intellectual transition. Big surprise, huh? Transition is what the preteen years are all about, and the way they think and learn is no exception.

What is wrong with this child?

Since so much of a preteen's life revolves around formal education, the effects on schoolwork are noticed—and evaluated—quickly. But the transitional disruption is deeper than academics.

One of our sons just loved to run errands for us. We could ask him to run downstairs and fetch a diaper for the baby, let the dogs out, be sure the back door was locked, and tell his big brother it was time to come upstairs.

"Yes, ma'am!" he'd respond, and dash off on his mission. We used to call him "our velociraptor" because he'd like to pretend to be a quick-moving dinosaur.

Then he turned eleven.

"Son, go get me my keys," one of us would tell him. The car keys were always left on top of the microwave oven in the kitchen. No variation.

Forty-five minutes later, we'd find him wandering aimlessly around the house. His shades were up, but no one was home.

It happened just the other day with one of our girls.

"Honey, go get me some water so I can take my medicine."

"Sure, Mom!" and she jumped up and left the room.

A few minutes later, she came back empty-handed.

"Honey, could you go get me some water?"

"Yes, ma'am!" and she left again.

Guess what? A few minutes later, she came back with no water. Melanie began to lose her cool.

"Could you *please* go get me some water, right now?!?"

"Mommy, I'm *glad* to help you," our daughter protested plaintively. "You don't have to be *harsh!*"

Clearly she had no clue that the question had ever been asked before.

This can get pretty exasperating. Moms often write us for support in disciplining their forgetful kids, sure that it's disobedience or rebellion, "since they had no problems doing those things last year!" The fact is, it's not as simple as that. The crazy absentmindedness and distraction of this age often can't be helped.

During puberty, the part of the brain changing the most is the area that controls executive functions. These are tasks like problem solving, priority setting, short term memory, attention, and focus. This is the center of common sense and good judgment, the part which decides, "This thing—Good idea? Bad idea?" It's the part which is plainly dormant when your twelve-year-old shouts, "Hey Mom! Watch *this!*"

Neurologists say that during early adolescence, these parts of the brain actually unravel; there truly is a temporary loss of function as the neurons re-assemble into their adult configurations. This explains a lot, doesn't it?

You might have looked at your preteen recently and thought or said, "I don't know what's wrong with you. You were able to do this without help last year. Your younger siblings can do it, why can't you?" It's because their brains are truly a bit scrambled right now. Kids that could concentrate and remember what they were doing last year suddenly can't, once the hormones start flowing. They *can't.*

So, how do you cope with this child who wakes up one day and their brain seems to stay in bed?

First, with patience. They will need more reminders and more supervision until they get through this. It's frustrating that your eight-year-old is more dependable than your eleven-year-old at the moment, but it won't be forever.

We found we had to be sure and get their undivided attention—full eye contact!—and then have them clearly repeat back the instruction you just gave them. Use their name. And still, don't be surprised if they forget before they arrive where you sent them. You can encourage them to really clear their mind of any distraction and rehearse the request until they've completed it.

"Going to get the car keys... I'm going for car keys... must get the car keys..."

And you, dear parent, repeat to yourself, "It's going to get better... it's going to get better..."

Your ten o'clock scholar

Often the first sign that things are changing upstairs is when schoolwork falls apart—or at least gets a lot harder. Ask anyone about middle school. You can just expect kids to stumble at this point.

While most of us know we need to prepare our children for the physical changes, this is an area that we need to talk about as well. If your child has sailed through the early years of school, that first bit of broken pavement may put him completely in the ditch.

One of our sons showed natural aptitude for math, and since homeschoolers aren't locked into a fixed curricular schedule—frankly, they were the first to practice "no child left behind" as a teaching philosophy—we thought we'd let him just run free. If he finished Grade 1 early, go ahead and start Grade 2. Just how far could he go, if he didn't have to wait for the rest of the class to catch up?

So naturally, after a few years of this, he was well ahead of his age-mates in the schools. By ten years old he was already two years ahead of grade level. And then the puberty brain-fade hit. And at the same time, the reality of cognitive development kicked it.

One of the key steps at this age is the development of abstract reasoning skills. These aren't critical for basic, or even advanced, arithmetic, but algebra is impossible without them. So at this point, our high-flying young arithmetician hit the mountainside of his own brain stage, and we didn't know that happened. For the first time, the concepts just weren't sinking in. He was confused, we were confused, and everyone was unhappy.

He rapidly concluded, then informed us, "I'm just no good in math."

The fact is, in a few more months, his brain began to function on a more adult level, and he was able not only to finish every level of high school math, but go on to calculus before he graduated. In college, he completed a degree in economics with plenty of calculus at that level, too, and yet to this day he avers, "I'm no good at math."

Our son may have had a self-confidence issue in this area, but he managed to overlook it and accomplish all his goals moving forward. Yet for many middle schoolers, that first hard patch causes them to throw in the towel for *all* academics. Trouble in math is just one subject, but deciding "I'm no good at *school*" can hinder them for life.

This is particularly detrimental for boys. Girls and boys develop differently in the early years, too, and the skills which come easiest to girls are the very things which are valued in the classroom. Most girls are able to sit still longer, they are more focused on pleasing the teachers, and frankly, most classroom teachers are former girls themselves; many naturally find it easier to manage the female students than the males.

What's more, girls are faster to develop small motor skills, the hand-eye coordination needed to write legibly and stay within the lines, so to speak. Boys develop other skills before the girls do—large motor skills and spatial reasoning are seen earlier with the boys—but those don't translate to classroom success quite so easily.

So by the time they hit the middle school slump, the girls may have some good experiences in reserve, to encourage them to persevere through whatever difficulties may have arisen. They're used to success and liked school before, so there's hope to regain that good feeling again.

But at the same time, many boys have been struggling for four or five years already. A setback at this point may be the last straw for some of them, and they can easily conclude, "Academics are not for me."

The sad part of this is that intellectually, boys accelerate coming out of the middle school years. While their sisters ran ahead of them in elementary school, the rapid development of academic processes stabilizes in the girls during this transition, while the boys' brains are awakening out of their doldrums. Boys as a group will often catch up any differences in their academic performance as compared to the girls in their class during high school.

But it won't happen if the boys decide to invest their interest and efforts elsewhere in the fifth or sixth grades.

Saving the love of learning

It's amazing to watch this late blooming in young men; we've seen it happen in our own home. One of our sons who struggled with dyslexia in his early years was beginning to lose hope for *any* future success by the time he reached middle school—and we his parents weren't sanguine about it, either. Yet while he continued to work with his learning disability, he grew so much intellectually that by his senior year, he was studying ancient philosophy for fun, and he went to college on a full-expense *academic* scholarship. It can be that dramatic!

For our guys and girls to get there, though, they have to try. To try, they have to have hope it's going to make a difference. They have to have an interest in learning. That means that one of your primary goals for the education of your preteens needs to be preserving their love of learning. Needless to say, that's a battle when they are struggling so much.

One way to help them is to recognize and remind them that learning is not the same as "school." Their level of education is more than a count of how many worksheets were finished and how many textbooks completed.

Their own experience should teach them this, but you may need to point it out. It's not unusual for a preteen to latch on to a subject or hobby almost to the point of obsession. We know middle-schoolers who independently, with no assignment or reward given, dove into library research, wrote to authors and authorities, read voraciously, and became quite expert in a specific area they loved.

One of our sons developed a fascination with falcons and other raptors; we don't live in the country, and the closest we'd ever get to these birds of prey was occasional red-tailed hawk sightings on the way to a nearby city. Yet he delved so deeply into the subject that on one magic day when a field trip introduced him to an actual falconer, the trainer was so amazed by the boy's knowledge he immediately opened a door to train him as a student.

You can leverage this sort of fascination to help them learn other subjects. Give them math problems relevant to their favorite subject. Use their pet topic as a springboard for creative writing exercises. Let them research the history of their hobby, or conjecture its future. Introduce them, if you can, to knowledgeable people in the field. Look up the science of their interests and help them grow even *more* understanding of a subject they already love.

Another benefit of this quest is that you open a door to a deeper relationship with your child. A parent who shows an interest in something precious to the child can leave a lasting impression far beyond the parent's imagination. In the emotional turmoil of this age, it is too easy for the child to feel isolated and imagine himself unloved or herself disregarded. When a parent engages the same things that have engaged their child, though, the child finds an unexpected connection—and a point of stability amid the storm.

The speed bump in their heads

Another bump in the road they face is the transition to abstract thinking. This is critical to the next phase of math. Some precocious children who've gotten ahead of their grade level in math sometimes suddenly start struggling when they hit pre-algebra—just like our son. The hormones have to do their job in developing abstract reasoning ability before algebra, trigonometry, or other higher math is even possible. That's one reason that, if you have an intellectually gifted child, you might not want to push them ahead too far in math.

When our son just raced ahead, we didn't know any better than to encourage it. When he got to a certain point, though, this boy who had never struggled in math before in his life just hit a wall. It got *hard*. It really shook him and he decided, "I'm no good at math." He still thought he was no good at math long after he'd conquered college calculus. It would have been better, when he needed more challenge in elementary school, to broaden and expand his education rather than push it ahead. Now, we generally suggest people keep younger children within a year or so of their grade level until they hit that mental growth spurt that opens the cognitive door for upper level math.

Another technique which can help a struggling learner is to teach what you are teaching. Some teachers like to combine skills as much as possible, as an integrated sort of learning. Unfortunately, this can backfire.

A mother told us at a conference, "My son hates science."

That was a surprising statement, especially concerning the generalized sort of science taught before high school. Most boys we've known may not have been ready for laboratory research, but they loved learning about rocks, animals, machinery, and chemical reactions.

When we dug a little deeper, we found that this homeschooling mother, like some classroom teachers, was requiring her son to answer the end-of-chapter questions in longhand, writing full sentences with proper grammar and spelling, and so forth. It became clear that her son didn't hate *science*—he was struggling with *writing*.

While the idea of layering subjects like that has some logic, it may not be a good idea at younger ages, and even in some cases with middle schoolers. For a student struggling with dyslexia or the related problem of dysgraphia—difficulty with handwriting, expecting him or her to answer science and history questions as if they were exercises in English composition may be as frustrating as requiring your math students to answer word problems presented in Russian.

On the other hand, unit studies which allow kids to study the same topic across the curriculum can be very motivating to tweens. They are beginning to make connections across subjects, and discussions can be very fruitful. The goal is to spread the fun and motivation across all of school; just don't extend difficulties in writing or math to the rest of school, though.

During the preteen years, your child may also need more supervision and fewer distractions. That may look different with different children at different times. Sometimes they may need to work in another room, listening to music on earbuds in order to concentrate. Other times, they may need to sit right next to you to keep from being distracted. Do what works.

One way to motivate them to do their schoolwork is to help them understand the usefulness of what they're learning. Teaching them how these tools are used in the real world helps. Show them how you would calculate the square footage of wall space minus the windows to find out how much paint to buy. Talk about how they'll need to understand the Word of God to teach it to their children. Explain how you use math to understand your finances.

An even greater motivation is to talk about what they're going to do with their lives. At this age, their goals are not likely to be very realistic or sensible. They might say they want to be game programmers, rocket scientists, or ballerinas. As hard as it might be, take them seriously for the moment. Actually look into what it would take to do those things. Explain how they'll have to learn their math and English to make those goals happen.

School makes a lot more sense when you realize it's your launching pad to accomplish what you dream. Best of all is when the student takes on responsibility for himself; "It's my life to live, and I need to get as much preparation as I can before I leave high school!" But to be fair, that would be a rare middle schooler indeed—let's celebrate the student who reaches high school with his interest and enthusiasm high!

Half-baked ideas

Some of the changes of this transition are exciting to watch. As the analytic faculties take root, students begin to make connections between different subjects. A history lesson might be interrupted by a sudden realization from science class, "Whoa! So disease killed more soldiers than the fighting, because the doctors didn't really understand bacteria yet, right?" They might realize that Beethoven's symphonies were new and radical music in the time of Napoleon. They start to understand how Darwin's theories of random evolution in biology served to uncouple many political movements from a Biblical worldview—and contributed to genocide of supposedly "subhuman" people in the twentieth century.

Their ability to analyze information logically is growing quickly during early puberty. If you thought four-year-olds asked a million questions, brace yourself for this age. "Why?" is a central part of the preteen vocabulary.[2]

There is a balancing reality to this, though. As the young person feels this dawning understanding, he's likely to form his own theories and deliver the most startling pronouncements. They can be very sure of themselves and their remarkable new logical ability, and now that they can *really* understand the world, they'll explain it to you.

The difficulty is they have new tools, but not much material to work on. Understanding life and the cosmos takes time and experience, and much of the explaining they want to attempt requires judgment and perspective which comes with increasing maturity. Their inexperience can be hilarious and at the same time, frustrating.

In many situations of this age and the one that follows, the wise parent may find himself moving from the position of director to coach. This is one of those situations; when a young philosopher erupts with a completely untenable dictum, you might take the opportunity to discuss it—quietly—with her, and calmly show her where she may have incomplete knowledge or inaccurate reasoning.

But if the preteen's in the middle of an emotional storm—for example, explaining exactly why the world is wrong and everyone hates him personally—you're probably going to have to wait it out or calm them down before correcting their mistaken intellectual conclusions.

---

[2] Susan Wise Bauer, "What Is Classical Education?" *The Well-Trained Mind*. Peace Hill Press, n.d. Web. 31 Mar. 2016. http://www.welltrainedmind.com/classical-education/.

Laying foundations for high school

I n our webinar series where we talk through these issues, the session on education includes thoughts on high school and beyond. It's not surprising when the parents of a wildly-gyrating 11-year-old shake their heads in disbelief. When finishing sixth-grade seems just remotely possible, the idea of planning for Grade 12 is just too much to comprehend.

Yet the fact is, the preteen years transition into the teen years very soon, and that means high school. High school in turn will transition to college or military or career or other adult choices.

And the decisions you make when they're ten years old may have an effect on the sort of college they apply to, or the job training program they enter, or any of a world of other doorways at age 18.

So now that this thoroughly frightening prospect is out in the open, let's remember that there's still a lot of time and opportunity before they reach for their high school diploma. How can you make the best of the years right now, to better prepare for the years ahead?

Catch up where necessary

T he middle school years and their built-in pauses in the curriculum are a great time to get your kids caught up before the challenges of high school (which, to be truthful, are sometimes themselves pulled back into the eighth—or even seventh grades).

If your students are still struggling with reading, you might find audiobooks a useful resource. Many textbooks are available in audio formats, and it's not hard to find literary works in audio.[3] With our struggling reader, we found that by listening to the older works read aloud, he could develop skill in grammar and vocabulary, as well

---

[3] We carry a collection of our favorites on our own site: http://raisingrealmen.com/shop

as processing the more complex sentences and paragraphs found in 19th-century and earlier writing. Besides that, he could learn other subject matter better from the audio experience, like history and geography. We also found the introduction to great authors prompted them to seek out those authors' other works, the ones which might not be on an audiobook download site. It's always easier to comprehend the spoken word than the written! The whole exercise improves reading comprehension as they learn to follow a complex thought through a paragraph, which can open doors to the printed word in turn. They learn what written language sounds like, and that will help them speed ahead when their decoding ability catches up.

If they are not reading comfortably by middle school, you are likely dealing with dyslexia, a problem processing the written word. One of our sons was still not reading by the time he was ten. We discovered a brain training program we could do at home, inexpensively, that revolutionized learning for him.[4] He went from reading on a first grade level to a college level in a couple of years.

Most parents have probably heard of dyslexia, but there are other learning glitches that may need attention during this time. We had a son whose reading comprehension was phenomenal—and he could read a 400-page novel in an evening with excellent recall—but whose handwriting was painfully slow, almost a physical pain to him. This condition is dysgraphia, and while it may appear with dyslexia, it can also appear as an independent condition like our son's.

Sometimes when you take the labor of handwriting out of the picture, a dysgraphic student will realize she really *can* "write"—that is, compose words to communicate verbally — after all. One option is to try letting your student dictate some of her compositions. Voice

---

[4] Dianne Craft's materials for struggling learners are excellent for kids struggling in reading, writing, listening, or attention. You can find them on our site at http://raisingrealmen.com/product-category/struggle

recognition software is becoming easier and easier to use (and many of us use it on our cell phones every day now).

Even substituting a keyboard instead of a pen or pencil may free up your student to create and express. Our dysgraphic son, for whom a three-paragraph essay was as much effort as re-writing *War and Peace*, received a used laptop from an uncle who was upgrading his office equipment. That fall, he entered a novel writing contest and completed over 15,000 words in a month.[5]

Eventually they will need to push an implement across paper, under timed-testing conditions; written questions are a real possibility, even for the non-academic young adult. But let handwriting be handwriting, and other subjects be true to themselves (science, history, math, and so forth), while you address any learning challenges your child may still have.[6]

Math is a struggle for many kids this age. Moms complain about their children spending three hours doing math. *We've* complained about *our kids* taking three hours doing math! They can't pay attention, they lose focus, they're easily distracted. Of course, they are; their executive functions aren't working properly. The question is, what can you do to help them through it?

We discovered that timing them can give a little bit of stress they need to focus. This seems counterintuitive to many women, for whom stress tends to be its own distraction. For men, though, a moderate amount of stress will actually focus their thought processes; this is probably why a woodworker or mechanic may grit his teeth or bite the inside of a lip when concentrating on a precise measurement or adjustment.

---

[5] For comparison, *The Great Gatsby* and *The Old Man and The Sea* were both about 25,000 words long. Fifteen thousand words is nothing to sneeze at!

[6] See footnote 4 above for help with these learning glitches.

When our young mathematicians began to hit the wall, time wise, we have put a stopwatch on their problem sets. We might start off by observing, "Son, yesterday you took two hours and fifteen minutes to finish your homework for this subject. If you can beat that time today, I'll give you a treat!"

It's surprising how small a reward will motivate boys. It may be a cookie or a tiny box of raisins or a single piece of candy. For boys, it seems, food is great, but *winning* is the real reward.

Remarkably, it's never failed—as soon as we began keeping time, the student's performance improves. We don't make it higher stress than necessary—no dramatic countdowns like a TV gameshow—but simply give a half-way reading like "You're on the right pace," or "You need to pick it up a little." Over as little as a week, we've seen a child go from two hours, nearly three, down to a consistent forty-five minutes for the same sort of problem set.

One special challenge we've used is to make sure he's memorized and really digested his basic math facts. A foreign language teacher told Hal that it was no good for a student of his to be standing on a street corner in a foreign city, conjugating. The same is true for math, especially the basic facts which a middle schooler should know. If the times table is familiar backwards and forwards, if the steps for long division are familiar, and the basics of handling fractions are well-understood, then the student can focus their full attention on new concepts—not "stand around" figuring out basic multiplication again.

We make a game out of the "fact sheets" used to drill for this comprehension. We'll make copies and pass them around to the whole family—both parents included!—and try to complete 100 examples in five minutes. It's a race against each other, but we reward "personal best" times at any level—again, some minimal reward is fine.

Once they've mastered 100 in five minutes, students seem to turn a corner and become even more skilled. The five minute mark is the point when they finally have the facts memorized, and it doesn't take but a few days more to get below three minutes for the same sheet.

Once they've done that, math in general gets much faster, and that's a relief to all of us.

There is hope here, too

Thankfully, the day comes when they start coming out of this phase. For several of our guys, it started with them asking if we minded if they got up early.

"Well, what are you planning to do?"

"I thought that if I got up early, I could do my chores and school early and have the rest of the day free."

When we recovered consciousness, we agreed that was a great idea!

Seriously, it's pretty amazing when they start getting their heads together again. When they start using those new intellectual abilities and maturity to become more responsible and more self-directed. What a relief!

Many A Conflict, Many A Doubt

4

"Mom, I think I'm an atheist," announced our nine-year-old from the back of the van one sunny day.

Melanie nearly drove into the ditch. This was the child we had prayed over since the day he was conceived. We'd sung hymns as lullabies and read the Bible to him from birth. He had memorized Scripture and the Q&A from the children's catechism nearly from the time he could talk. We spoke about Biblical truth and God's commandments and salvation by faith on a daily basis. We were delighted to see him role-playing Bible stories with his younger brother, and he had sat with us in "big people" worship services from infancy onward.

In other words, we'd done everything we knew to teach him God's truth and invite him to embrace it. And before he turned ten, it seemed, we were about to lose him.

The most disturbing change

Of all the changes we meet in the preteen years, this one has to be the most disturbing for Christian parents. The others are plenty disruptive—the emotional volatility, the academic doldrums, the "juvenile senility"—but the sudden possibility of losing your son or daughter to "the world, the flesh, and the devil" before their twelfth birthday, in spite of your best efforts and earnest prayer…*that* is both heartbreaking and terrifying.

It's doubly disconcerting when you look back on their earlier childhood. Many children seem to reach a spiritual awareness in their elementary years. One of the churches Hal grew up in assumed that baptized children were ready to become practicing members of the church when they reached six years old. To be sure, we've seen several of our own children of that age apparently wake up to the fact that an unseen God and Savior are nevertheless *real*. They came to us with the sweetest professions of faith in Jesus—and without any leading questions or undue prompting from us. We only *pointed* them to the Lord—we didn't push, pull, or drag them there.

So it's discouraging, to say the least, to see a child who seemed to trust the Lord at age six, suddenly developing doubts or even skepticism at ten or eleven. It's almost as if the preschooler thinks, "Mom and Dad love Jesus, and I want to love Him too!" but the preteen thinks in turn, "Wait a minute—how can they be so sure?"

What about that childlike faith?

The way we think about this issue will be shaped by our theological framework, of course. If you come from a church which believes that true salvation can be lost and regained, once or many times, then there may be no conflict in your mind over the idea that a child may be born again at age six and lost again at age nine.

Many evangelical churches teach some form of eternal security—in other words, that a true believer will continue in faith till death. If you have this expectation, it can be a shock when a child seems to turn back on his earlier profession. What happened—both then, and now? And what should we do about it?

Dennis Gundersen, the author of *Your Child's Profession of Faith*, brings nearly thirty years of pastoral experience to the question. He says that it is quite possible for a very young child to be genuinely saved and truly born again—he's known some as young as three who seemed to have a real faith that grew and matured as they grew up.

The difficulty he identifies for parents and pastors is that a child's *salvation* is separate from her *profession of faith*. It's easy for a young person to say the right things without really understanding what they're about, so we shouldn't be too confident of their spiritual condition based on the child's words alone. Since we humans can't truly know another person's innermost heart, we have to rely on external signs of God's work in their soul. Sometimes, admittedly, it's hard to be sure.

So how should we think about our young child's early belief?

It's possible we were mistaken about our child's first claim of faith. Maybe they were repeating things they'd heard from others, or wanted to be included in something they didn't understand yet, or maybe they were seeking approval from parents or teachers who had celebrated other children's professions of faith. When they later hit a new way of thinking about spiritual matters, they may have naturally backed away from an earlier decision.

Or it could be we weren't mistaken at all. It may be that the younger child really was a repentant sinner saved by grace. This time of new questions and doubts is not a preteen rejection of the faith, but a desire to *work out your own salvation with fear and trembling*.[1] They have a new capacity to consider, analyze, and compare, and they may be true believers who just want to be sure. For the first time, they may be trying to think about faith the way an adult would.

---

[1] Philippians 2:12b (ESV)

Gundersen says that true belief results in a change of heart and a change of life, whether the new believer is five years old, fifteen, or fifty. He counsels parents to be hopeful for their child who professes to believe, pray for them to grow in God's grace, but keep sharing the basics of repentance and faith until there is clear external evidence of a changed heart.

Doubts are normal

At the time of his surprise announcement, we didn't know our son's spiritual doubts were pretty normal.

It makes sense if you think about the physical and emotional changes and uncertainties of this age. Preteens are experiencing emotional swings that make them feel angry, sad, alone, and unloved. Meanwhile their intellects are changing and growing. They begin to understand that not everyone believes like their parents. They begin to question if what they've been taught is true, including the spiritual parts. Spiritual doubts, second thoughts, and hesitations can only be expected.

As alarming as this is to a Christian parent, this time of questioning can actually be a very good thing—if handled properly. At some point, believing in Jesus has to be more than just "because Mommy and Daddy said so." Real faith has to rest on an individual's own relationship to God. This is the time that your children can make their faith their own.

The stakes are pretty high. The Gen2 Survey studied almost 10,000 adults 18 to 34 who were raised in Christian homes. Many of those who walked away from the faith as adults, first had doubts in the middle school years. Having doubts is not unusual as a preteen or young teen. If unaddressed, though, those questions can grow into full blown rejection of God.[2]

Our friend, Carol Barnier, author of *Engaging Today's Prodigal*, lived that story. She began having spiritual doubts in middle school, but as a pastor's daughter, she was afraid her questions would break her parents' hearts. Instead, she internalized them, playing along with the expectations of a preacher's kid in church, Sunday school, and youth group...all while the doubts wormed deeper into her thinking.

When she got to college, she found people who had answers for her doubts—the wrong answers, but they seemed to make sense. Carol became a literal card-carrying atheist for 12 years, joining an association and working to destroy the faith of others. Eventually, she came to Christ through the testimony of believers willing to address her questions and discuss hard issues with her.

Wouldn't it be better to deal with these doubts when they're new and small?

Don't freak out

A helpful principle for parenting through any age is the simple reminder, "Don't Freak Out." After all, God assigned *us* to be the parents of *these* particular children, at *this* point in history, and so on. The challenges that arise in our homes arrive with His full knowledge and plan, so even the startling things which appear with our preteen children are part of the program. That means we can look to Him for help—and we shouldn't panic.

If your kids are struggling with doubts, you really should welcome them bringing their concerns to you. Carol Barnier got her questions answered elsewhere, at a great cost. The Internet is an endless source

---

[2] Brian D. Ray, *Gen 2 Survey: A Spiritual and Educational Survey on Christian Millennials.*

of bad advice. Wouldn't you rather be their first source instead of Google?

But if you hope to have your children confide their worries and problems to you, that means you can't overreact. They need to feel that they have permission to ask questions and confidence their parent won't faint, have a stroke, or put them on house arrest until they turn thirty.

If your child blurts out something like our son did, a good response (after a deep breath) is, "What makes you say that?"

Then listen to what they are really saying. It's hard to hear the child you've prayed for all his life, that you've poured the Bible into, that you've taken to church week after week, now questioning the most important truths in your life. You may feel betrayed or rejected. You may be terrified at the possible outcome, but you *need* to understand what your child is thinking and feeling. So listen.

Then address what's worrying him. Often the questions are basic, foundational matters that are assumed in most of our daily life. How can we know there really is a God? How do we know the Bible is true? Aren't there many ways to heaven?

You might be solid in your own faith, but uncomfortable making a sustained argument for the evidence supporting Christianity. The field of apologetics is the study of how to defend the faith—how do you give an answer for what you believe? And some questions *are* difficult to answer off the cuff.

We have a reasonable faith that can stand up to examination. We don't need to be afraid of our children's honest questions. Instead, we should welcome them as an opportunity to help ground them in the truth. There's no question your child might ask that hasn't been asked before, and our inability or unwillingness to deal with contrary ideas may cause more trouble than the original question. It's okay to say, "That's a good question. Let's go find out!"

Some of the most fundamental questions have fairly straightforward explanations from Scripture and simple logic. Your son might ask, "How do we even know there's a God?"

"That's a great question, Son," you might say, "and there are a lot of ways to answer. I think one of the best is to look at the world around us. Nothing seems to happen without a cause. Plants and animals and people don't just appear—they exist because something caused them. Chickens come from eggs, which are laid by earlier chickens, which grew from earlier eggs, and so on. Sooner or later you have to ask—How did it start? Why was there a chicken ever? Or a first egg? The reason is that Someone greater than chickens had the power to make a chicken from nothing. That's the Creator—God. And He created so much more than just chickens."

Your daughter might ask about the popular notion that there are many ways to heaven. You might respond, "Honey, you remember the jailer in Philippi who asked, *'What must I do to be saved?'* And the apostles told him, *'Believe in the Lord Jesus Christ, and you will be saved.'*[3] They didn't say anything about being a good man or offering sacrifices or walking in obedience to whatever religion you like. It was one thing only—believing in Jesus and putting your trust in Him for salvation. Jesus Himself said, *'I am the way, the truth, and the life; no one comes to the Father except through Me.'*[4] You can't get clearer than that; Jesus is the only way to God and heaven."

Your pastor is a great source of help in answering those hard questions. He'd almost certainly welcome an opportunity to put his studies to use in that way. You can ask him for advice on how to answer specific

---

[3] Acts 16:30-31
[4] John 14:6

questions, or his recommendations for books and resources, or you might suggest a casual meeting with you and your child over lunch to address some of these issues.

Often you need to help your children dig a little deeper for themselves, too. Maybe you can study a book together. We've read *Mere Christianity* by C.S. Lewis with all of our teens so far. It's a good, extensive explanation of how we can know God exists and that He's revealed Himself in the Christian Bible. At different times, we've looked into books which dealt with more detailed evidence, like Ken Ham's *Evolution: The Lie,* Josh McDowell's *Evidence That Demands a Verdict,* or Lee Strobel's *The Case for Christ.* By the early teens, most are ready to deal with philosophical ideas—in fact, they crave them.

When Melanie was a teenager, her high school organized a debate between an evolutionary biologist and a creationist. The evolutionist was overconfident of his argument and spent his hour alternating between bald assertions of his position and laughing at the creationist viewpoint. To his dismay, the creationist came with a well-prepared argument and plenty of evidence, and the more professional presentation won the day, hands down.

Melanie remembers being flooded with relief, thinking, "I can be intellectually honest and still be a Christian!" It was a turning point in her life.

It also underscores an important fact—if your preteen is asking questions, she may not be saying, "I'm skeptical—prove it!" Instead, she might be joining the desperate father in the Gospels to cry out, "*I believe—help my unbelief!*"[5] Challenging a key doctrine or raising a philosophical objection may your child's way of saying, "I recognize a question here, and I can't see my way through it. Can you help me?"

---

[5]   Mark 9:24

Not my child!

Sometimes parents will tell us their children have made it to the teen years and haven't voiced any doubts at all. Since questioning and uncertainty is so common at this age, it's safest to assume that doubts have at least occurred to your preteen, whether or not he mentions them. They may be relieved if you bring up the questions for them.

This happens in other areas. One of our sons was very uncomfortable thinking about medical questions, but was all ears when we discussed them with his brother. Some don't want to admit they're confused, or they just want to think their questions through on their own. Some kids don't bring up their doubts because they don't want to disappoint you or make you angry. You need to let them know that you *want* to talk about this stuff with them.

If your child is not boiling over with spiritual questions, you might stir the pot a bit by proposing one of your own. You might say something like, "I remember when I was your age, I really wondered how we knew the Bible was inspired by God and trustworthy to believe. Have you ever thought about that?" Ask yourself what questions you struggled with when you were a preteen or young teen.

Book studies are a great way to deal with the quiet doubter or even the child who professes to be "just fine," but leaves you wondering whether they really are. "Let's read this book as a family this month" or "Let's you and I read a chapter of this each week and we'll discuss it over ice cream" are good approaches.

You might also choose to study particular books of the Bible as part of family devotions. Romans, Ephesians, and Colossians are great doctrinal books that cover a lot of territory. Galatians is our go-to book for discussing the difference between grace and law, between faith and legalism. The gospel of Matthew shows how Jesus of Nazareth was the complete fulfillment of the Messianic prophecies. If you're not comfortable pulling doctrinal lessons out of the Word yourself, you can use a commentary or devotional guide to help with the discussion; ask your pastor for recommendations if you need to.[6]

Whatever path you take, don't let your son or daughter quietly drift until they're seventeen or eighteen and only then find out they've lost their faith and don't know where to turn. At that point, you'll have very little time to help them before they are out on their own.

True conversion

The son that announced he was an atheist didn't stay that way very long. One evening, after a few months and a great deal of discussion, study, prayer, and dealing with sin, he announced out of the blue, "Mama, I think I'm going to go crazy if I don't trust God to save me!"

At that moment, the baby started screaming upstairs. Since Hal was working late and hadn't made it home yet, Melanie told our son, "Look, I have to go to the baby, but I'll be done as soon as I can. You know what you need to do. Talk to God about it."

When the baby calmed down, Melanie hurried anxiously downstairs. As soon as she walked in the room, she saw a new light in our son's eyes. It had been settled between him and God while Mom was out of the room, and he's followed Christ consistently ever since, even as an adult. If you're confronted with a case of preteen doubt, take it seriously, but don't take it as God's final word in that young life!

---

[6] Our favorite commentary is Matthew Henry's *Commentary on the Whole Bible*. Since the early 1700's, this very readable work has been a standard reference for students, teachers, and pastors for centuries, and with good reason!

The Awakening   5

S everal years ago, when we gave our basic talk about raising
sons, we had one slide which talked about sexuality and
purity. We usually spent about three minutes on it; the talk
was comprehensive and we had lots of other ground to cover.

To our surprise, though, that one short passage invariably prompted
comments.

"We're *very* careful about what we let our son watch," the mother
would say. "We don't watch network television and we carefully
screen every video we show."

"Of course," we'd agree.

"And we pre-read any books we bring home," she'd continue.
"Certainly!" we'd say.

"I just don't want to put evil thoughts in his head," she'd conclude.

"Of course not," we'd say. "So how old is your son?" we'd ask, expecting
to hear maybe six or seven.

"Fourteen," she'd say.

One told us "Seventeen." Melanie told her, in her sweetest Southern-
lady voice, that at that age her son was so full of testosterone, he would
be having trouble with his thoughts on a desert island all by himself.

It's later than you think

P arents never really like to think that their children need to hear about sexuality as young as they do. If you're thinking about your ten—or eleven-year-olds, they may not have hit their growth spurt yet. They may look like big children, but they are still unmistakably *kids*.

Parents frequently tell us they don't want to introduce the subject, because they're afraid it will steal their children's innocence. We understand that and we sympathize, but the world has changed since we were kids ourselves, and children are being exposed to sexually charged messages far sooner than we might think.

The realization that lots of parents were in some sort of denial about their children's developing sexual awareness prompted us to offer to speak on the subject at homeschool conventions. It was a very reluctant offer; we had young children at home and didn't want to be known as "the parents who stand up and talk about sex to rooms full of strangers." It was embarrassing to suggest, and embarrassing to do.

Yet the first time we gave that workshop, over four hundred parents packed into the hall. The second time, at a different event, there were at least *eight* hundred in a room set up for much less. People were seated on the floor around the stage, sometimes actually behind the projection screen. Clearly there was a need to address!

When you start teaching on a subject, you will discover more about it. When we first began talking about sexuality and boys, parents would come up afterward, concerned that they'd found their sixteen-year-old accessing inappropriate pictures on the internet. A few short years later, people are coming to us concerned about seven—to nine-year-olds they've caught watching explicit videos.

Yes, children that young. A 2010 study showed that a third of children are first exposed to internet porn before the age of ten.[1] We suspect things have gotten worse since then. It's natural for parents to think, "Well, not *my* child," but when over 90% of boys and nearly 60% of girls are exposed by the age of eighteen, there isn't much room for that assumption.

Pornography is nothing new. Archaeologists uncover lewd drawings on the walls of ancient cities. Grecian urns and Roman artwork reveal far too much about what went on behind closed doors. Chaplains walking the battlefields of the Civil War found soldiers who didn't die immediately from their wound often passed away some time later with a Testament or rosary in their hands; others were found clutching pornographic postcards in their stiff dead fingers.

A generation ago, kids who wanted to peek at dirty pictures could usually find a sketchy uncle who kept his "men's magazines" in the garage, or an older brother who was careless what he brought home from college, or a friend who was brazen enough to shoplift a magazine from the drugstore. Video was much harder to access, but the printed trash was easy enough to find.

Now the porn is accessible from everyone's cell phone. If you say, "That's why my child doesn't have one," it doesn't prevent their friends from sharing pictures (the same way they used to share the magazines). And the access to video is a total revolution; over 80% of boys and 50% of girls have seen videos of group sex, nearly 70% of boys and more than 50% of girls have seen homosexual acts online, and many have seen things that we're uncomfortable even mentioning.

---

[1] Unless stated otherwise, all statistics in this chapter from *Porn Stats: 250+ Facts, Quotes, and Statistics About Pornography Use*. (Owosso, MI: Covenant Eyes, 2015).

What's more, the porn media culture has become personally dangerous. In one study, 60% of kids said they had been asked for an explicit photo or video of themselves. The news regularly reports on teens who were driven to suicide over their sexual messages they'd sent that were used to blackmail or intimidate them.

Sexuality is not something we can wait to talk about after they're shaving. In fact, despite our best efforts, it's likely they'll be exposed sometime in the preteens, if not before. This is an issue we need to face up to.

The battle is lasting longer

T he God who created our sexual nature created marriage as the context for expressing it and as a protection against immorality—once we're wedded. That is becoming a problem in our society.

Until the 1970s, men in our society generally married in their early twenties (22 or 23 was average), and women a few years younger (19 or 20 on average). Since 1970, though, that statistic has been climbing—dramatically. Now just a generation later, the average age of first marriage has risen to nearly 27 for women and over 29 for men. The time when a young person reaches that God-ordained destination has moved later and later in life.

At the same time, the onset of puberty—and sexual awareness—is coming earlier and earlier. In 1860, girls were beginning puberty between sixteen and seventeen, and boys about a year later.[2] Now, girls often reach puberty between eight and ten and boys between nine and eleven. Ponder that for a minute: in the past 150 years, the length of physiological childhood has been cut in half.

---

[2] McKie, Robin. "Onset of Puberty in Girls Has Fallen by Five Years since 1920." *The Guardian.* Guardian News and Media, 20 Oct. 2012. Web. 03 Apr. 2016. <http://www.theguardian.com/society/2012/oct/21/puberty-adolescence-childhood-onset>.

No one is entirely sure why this radical change has happened. Health and nutrition definitely play a role. There are more hormones in the food stream and bioactive chemicals in plastics and other environmental factors. Whatever the cause, sexual development is beginning much sooner than it used to.

These two trends mean that our young people are facing sexual temptation for a lot longer than teens used to. When people went through puberty at sixteen to eighteen and married at eighteen to twenty-two, there was only a short time of severe temptation without God's ordained provision. But when boys and girls are starting puberty at eight to twelve and marrying in their late twenties, they are facing nearly two decades of temptation.

Recognizing that our children are likely going through puberty earlier than we did and now face temptations like porn younger and more intensely than we did means that we need to step in and help them sooner than we might be comfortable.

A gift of God, often misused

Our sexual nature and the sexual act itself are gifts of God with a specific purpose and blessing. God created a man and a woman, Adam and Eve, and gave them to one another in marriage–a historic fact cited by both the Lord Jesus Christ and Paul the apostle.[3] The sexual act was created *before* sin entered the world, and first commandment recorded in the Bible is God's instruction to this first couple, "*Be fruitful and multiply,*"–in other words, to begin sexual relations.[4] And after God had made male and female, created the institution of marriage, and commanded them to be sexually

---

[3] Jesus, on marriage in Creation, Matthew 19:4-6. The Apostle Paul, Ephesians 5:31.
[4] Genesis 1:28

active and have children, the Bible tells us, *"God saw everything that He had made, and indeed, it was very good."*[5]

The problem we face in our world after Eden is that everything in Creation has been marred and distorted by human sinfulness. The very good and very powerful gift of sex has been stolen, abused, and sullied by sinful mankind. Our challenge is to protect our children from the misuse of sexuality and from sin, while preparing them for a healthy, joyful marital relationship.

Our enemy, Satan, is opposed to that entirely. We can see that in the culture. At one college we visited with our son, we saw a poster in the student center encouraging students to "Try Dating!" It listed dozens of innocent outings like a bike ride, a trip to the botanical garden, a walk in the quad, or a movie at the campus theater. Why would they be promoting this obvious activity? Because the modern campus culture has made commitment or even emotional attachment purely optional to sexual activity. Some in the Christian community have proposed a more formal courtship over dating, but in the hookup culture of American colleges, innocent dating would be a vast improvement over casual fornication. Romance and love are dead or passé in most universities, it seems.

Off campus, the majority of couples today are living together before marriage. Most children born to women under thirty are born out of wedlock. And that's just conventional decadence. The effort to redefine marriage and extend recognition to same-sex couples was crowned by the Supreme Court's *Obergefell* decision in the summer of 2016, but it was quickly leap-frogged by the redefinition of gender itself. Every day, we can watch a culture which has rejected God's order now tying itself in logical knots attempting to create a rational

---

[5] Genesis 1:31

society where gender is fluid and therefore meaningless—except when gender identity is the *most* important thing.

How much simpler, and honest, it is to simply accept God's definitions and guidelines about this most fundamental and intimate part of our humanity.

We live in the American South, in the states derisively called "the Bible Belt" for their large number of churches and open believers. Residents of more progressive cities and nations sometimes mock the traditional mores of conservative communities as a laughable, Puritanical construct, saying that sexual misbehavior (if such a thing exists) is no different than any other unhealthy or unkind habit.

Yet sexual sin is taken very seriously in the Word of God. There are dozens of commandments, warnings, and prohibitions against specific sexual sins, both in the Old and the New Testaments. The apostle Paul explicitly says that sexual sin is in a different category, as he warned the church in Corinth, "*Flee from sexual immorality. Every other sin a person commits is outside the body, but the sexually immoral person sins against his own body.*"[6]

Recent research has proven this to be literally true.

When we engage in sexual activity, our brain releases a reward hormone, dopamine, into the bloodstream; it's the trigger of the pleasant sensations we experience. Watching pornography causes a dopamine release, too (so do many other activities we find exciting). However, internet porn allows the user to witness far more sexual activity than is even possible in real life. This overstimulation causes the dopamine receptors to begin to desensitize, just like your pupils

---

[6] 1 Corinthians 6:18

contract when you walk into bright sunlight to protect your visual receptors.

That means the next time, to get the same thrill, the porn viewer must watch more intense, more exotic, or just *more* porn. Users are quickly drawn into more and more perverse material. They can become addicted to the dopamine surges, by the same mechanism that works in alcoholics, heroin addicts, or compulsive gamblers.

Jesus said that *"whosoever looks at a woman to lust for her has already committed adultery with her in his heart."*[7] The things in our mind and heart are important to the God who sees them both. Internet porn is a serious danger to our kids, one that can change their lives, weaken or destroy their marriages, and endanger their souls. We have to do what it takes to prepare them for this battle.

Not just visual porn, though

When looking at the lower statistics for girls and online porn, a parent might be tempted to think that if you have a daughter, you don't need to worry. It's true that girls aren't tempted by the same things as guys are, but they have temptations of their own.

One common trap for girls is what we call "story porn." Many of us remember the "bodice-ripper" sort of historical romances girls passed around when we were young. The book covers looked racy but just *barely* decent on the outside; inside we knew there were some pretty exciting scenes that we probably ought not to be reading. Of course, that was the attraction.

Many girls stumble into story porn through fan fiction. They read a book series they love and they hate when it comes to an end. Imagine

---

[7]   Matthew 5:28

their delight when they find lots more stories about those beloved characters online. The problem is there's no one curating the fan fiction. It doesn't have to meet a publisher's approval or satisfy a librarian before it reaches the public. Fan fiction ranges from badly written but harmless stories, to undeniably pornographic narratives.[8] It's a very real temptation to young women who are already emotionally tied to the characters.

The Word of God makes it plain that our hearts matter. Stirring up lust in our hearts is sin whether you are reading a story or looking at videos, whether it's seen with the eyes or the mind.

The talk?

Teaching preteens about sexuality and preparing them to fight temptation is not about one big, terrifying *Talk*, but an ongoing series of conversations from childhood until they are ready to marry. You give your toddlers and preschoolers the basic training about keeping their clothes on, acceptable and unacceptable touching, and warnings about strangers. During the preteen years, the conversation changes because your young person has changed. They begin to feel new desires and a burgeoning curiosity... and the capability to make life-changing decisions.

It may be uncomfortable for the parents, but we need to get more detailed and more serious about this conversation when our kids are starting adolescence. If you want your preteens to get a Biblical context for thinking about sexuality, you really *want* them to bring up awkward questions at home. If you don't want their views about sex to be totally shaped by the world's perspective, then you need to establish yourself in your child's eyes as the best and most reliable source of information about sex.

---

[8]   For instance, the sadomasochistic *Fifty Shades of Grey* series was originally *Twilight* series fan fiction. See the article in *Business Insider,* 17 Feb 2015.

We once received a counterfeit bill from an ATM. It looked passably like a twenty, but we could tell something wasn't right even without training. We'd seen enough of legitimate money that red flags went up. In fact, that's how banks train tellers to identify phony bills—by giving them lots of exposure to the real thing, not by showing examples of home-made currency.[9]

We want our children to have an understanding that sexuality is created by God and designed to be used only in the framework of love, commitment, marriage, and child-bearing. We want them to know that sex is good when it's enjoyed in the way God intends, and there's nothing shameful or guilty about it in that context. Conversations about sexuality, love, and relationships should be frank and frequent.[10]

When you've established this sort of conversation with your preteen, they'll immediately know it's phony when a neighbor or cousin tries to show them something "dirty." They'll know that something is wrong, and they'll also know the safest person to ask about it—Mom or Dad.

So when do they need to know details? How the plumbing works, so to speak? Unfortunately, that time comes way earlier than you think, if you want your children to hear it from you first — and you do. It doesn't have to be a big scene, and the discussion can happen pretty naturally. If you feel hopelessly embarrassed, invent a reason to go for a drive together at night. Talking in the car is great: you're both facing forward and you can't see each other blush in the dark. Just open the conversation, "Hey, I want to talk about some of the changes that are going to be happening soon in your body. God's

---

[9] Tim Challies, "Counterfeit Detection (Part 1)." *Challies.com: Informing the Reforming*, 27 Jun 2006

[10] For sons moving into the teen years, our book, *Love, Honor, and Virtue: Gaining or Regaining a Biblical Attitude Toward Sexuality* may help with this. (http://raisingrealmen.com/product/lhv)

preparing you to be a [woman or man]. Let's talk about how that happens."

It's important to give them details they might be tempted to seek elsewhere. Use the real words for body parts, not slang. A lot of fear and a lot of looking in the wrong places for answers can be prevented by parents who talk openly with their kids—even if they're dying of embarrassment.

Safety, more than ever

We all regret how our culture is robbing children of their innocence. The increasing sexualization of children is deplorable, and the growing use of pornography has made the world more dangerous for kids. In some cases, it has made the kids a danger to themselves and to other children.

One conservative Christian mother told us she was horrified to discover her teenaged son's phone contained pictures of his undressed siblings—and that he had been sharing them with friends. Even though he was legally a child himself, in many states the law defines this as trafficking in child pornography. Basically, a kid with a cell phone can become a pornographer. Many have.

How in the world would a child even think to do that? It starts with natural curiosity. This boy was curious about a word he didn't know, or maybe he clicked on an odd search result, or got drawn in by a sidebar link. You do not have to be a bad kid to find this stuff now; it comes looking for you. He found porn, and curiosity turned into a guilty habit. He watched more and more of it. He got drawn into worse and worse stuff. He found out his friends were watching, too, and they began to talk about it and share. Eventually, and tragically, they began to act out.

By intentionally working for a relationship of openness and trust in this area, we hope to head off the first steps down that path. If your children know you will calmly hear their questions and do your best to give clear, factual answers, they'll be less tempted to ask Mr. Search Engine. You *really* don't want your preteen to ask Mr. Search Engine—he's got pictures to share.

We need to teach our kids the boundaries for eyes and bodies—*specific* boundaries. We found a good, easy boundary is to say anything covered by their underwear or swimsuit is off limits. Nobody's allowed to touch them in those areas, they don't touch anyone else there, no show and tell, and photos are strictly *not allowed*. Every kid past diaper-age understands underwear, even if they don't change it like they ought to.

Tragically, the research shows that with the growth in pornography addiction and the increasing depravity of the media, child molestation is happening more and more. Unfortunately, we have to teach our children how to protect *themselves* from predators, because it's increasingly likely that someone they know may be tempted to turn their heart sin into physical sin.

We need to be alert to any sort of grooming behavior, such as adults taking an unexplained interest in one-on-one time with individual children. Be aware that many predators are excited by molesting children with their parents present. You need to be alert.

We especially need to tell our children that if someone threatens them, they need to tell you right away. Sometimes predators threaten the child, but sometimes the threat is against the child's parents, siblings, or pets. You need to make sure your kids know that you can take care of yourself and them, too.

With older kids, the threats change. Teens and preteens are often teased or dared into doing something stupid, then threatened with exposure to their friends, families, or schools if they don't cooperate in further sin. Some have even taken their lives rather than deal with the shame. Our kids need to know when they are dared that strong people aren't afraid to resist a taunt. It's the cowards who give in to do what they know is wrong or stupid, simply because they are afraid of their friends. The courageous do right no matter what people think.

Who's on the phone?

The apparent privacy of online communication can encourage kids to be bolder online than they ever would be in person. Like the unpleasant trolls who live in the comment boxes of news sites, young people may feel safe to do and say things through their phones and computers without thinking about the likely consequences.

Studies suggest that if you have three children, the likelihood is at least one of them will receive a sexually-explicit photo from a friend before they're out of high school. A recent analysis of 39 studies involving over 110,000 teens and preteens aged 12-17 found that nearly one in seven have sent sexual photos over their phones. Nearly one out of three has received a nude or nearly-nude image from a friend. The average age was 15.[11]

This suggests several matters of concern. Young kids still at home are creating inappropriate images of themselves and sharing them online. Sometimes, it's trying to attract attention from a romantic interest. Sometimes, it's because they were dared or even threatened

---

[11] Madigan S, Ly A, Rash CL, Van Ouytsel J, Temple JR. "Prevalence of Multiple Forms of Sexting Behavior Among Youth: A Systematic Review and Meta-analysis." *JAMA Pediatrics*. 26 Feb 2018

to do it. Either way, they are exposing themselves to an unknown and uncontrollable audience.

What's more, the difference between the 15% who send them and the 30% who receive them illustrates that these images are being shared beyond the romantic interest alone.

We've got to really impress our children that anything sent electronically is forever. Once it's released "into the wild," there's no calling it back. Even services that purport to show a photo only for a few seconds keep that photo on their own servers, and users quickly learn how to take a screenshot and save copies for their own purposes. What seems like a game between friends has life-long, real-world consequences. You only have to watch the news for a short time to see stories of students badgered, bullied, humiliated, or threatened over inappropriate pictures. Jilted boyfriends and girlfriends dump embarrassing photos onto social media as "revenge porn." And careers and reputations are being disrupted by the discovery of compromising pictures from years before.

The only way to prevent these sort of consequences is never create or participate. Just don't.

It's sad that we have to talk to our kids about things like this, but it's the world we're living in—and it's not improving.

Accountability is crucial

Remember the young man who got caught sending inappropriate pictures of his siblings? It didn't happen all at once. It was a long slide down the slippery slope. His mother told us regretfully, "I've heard you guys say again and again we needed to get accountability software on our phones and computers. We didn't know which one was best, though, so we never got around to it." Sadly, he didn't get caught until he had fallen so deeply into sin he had taken advantage of his younger siblings. The young man is responsible for his own sin, but his parents grieved that they hadn't taken steps to keep him safe.

Another mom told us she had read one of our articles about protecting children from porn and predators, and she thought she'd have a talk with her children. The mom was shocked when her thirteen-year-old *daughter* burst into tears. "Mommy, I've been watching that stuff for four months," she sobbed. "I've tried everything, but I can't stop!"

The mother told us her daughter had never been in a room alone with the computer. How could such a thing happen? The teen had been given permission to use her mom's laptop to look up something about her collectible dolls. When a strange search result came up, she clicked out of curiosity and soon was hooked. She'd been watching these videos in the living room, with her siblings playing around her. She'd even been lured into watching perversions that so horrified her she tried to quit, but wasn't able.

And the daughter was relieved when it all came out.

Having internet in our homes that isn't protected by blocking or accountability software is like dropping our kids off in the heart of a large city and saying, "We'll pick you up later!" Sure, there are museums, colleges, concert halls, and churches, but there are also predators, strip joints, and gambling dens. Get some kind of accountability software on every internet capable device in your home. Today. And keep in mind these are not solutions, but tools— you still need to be a vigilant parent and counselor to your kids.[12]

---

[12] Go to www.RaisingRealMen.com/safety for our latest recommendation. The link may include an affiliate code that supports our ministry.

Don't freak out

The most important protection your children have is a good relationship with you, their parents. Talking about sexuality is pretty embarrassing. We feel the same way. Getting over that embarrassment and becoming your child's first and best source of information is very worth it. It's an investment in his protection. You want to be the first resource that comes to his mind when he hears a word he doesn't know or something pops up on the screen he shouldn't see. Later, you want him to come right to you when his friends are suggesting sin to him or someone makes an inappropriate advance or he has questions as he prepares for marriage. That begins with a willingness to take a breath and respond calmly, when the question you just heard made your jaw drop or your face blush.

We had a discussion with one of our sons, a few months before his marriage. It was pretty frank, and we discussed a wide range of important issues about sexuality including things we wish we'd known when *we* got married. And *he* brought up the topic! We don't think that would have happened if we hadn't built a relationship of openness and trust over the years. Keep that in mind when they ask awkward questions when they're young—and don't freak out.

Social Struggles　6

Every year, our state homeschool conference holds a dance. It's a huge affair with hundreds of young people (and some parents, too) in one of the hotel ballrooms, with a professional dance caller teaching line-dancing steps and square dance patterns. It's strictly group stuff, lots of fun, and everybody looks forward to it.

Except for one of our sons who was going through this stage one year and announced he wasn't having any part of this event. No. Way.

"Can't I just stay here?" he demanded, back in the hotel room. "I don't want to go."

"No, I'd really like for you to go," Melanie replied. "Your brothers didn't want to go when they were your age, either, but they had fun. Didn't you guys?" His older brother chimed in with agreement and encouragement.

"I don't want to go," he insisted. "It'll be stupid. I don't know anybody there. Why do you care so much anyway?"

We knew he would have fun if he'd just try.

"Just go for an hour. If you don't like it, you can come back up to the room after that."

"I'm not going! I'm not going and you can't make me. You just hate me. You don't care how I feel. You don't care if I'm embarrassed!"

You can probably write the rest of the script yourself. Tears, yelling, and hysteria—all over a minor social event that we knew he'd probably enjoy. He'll get over this, we thought, if he'd only try it.

And he did—eventually. Just the other day, we looked on as that same son was happily dancing with a group of friends at a cookout, and encouraging a younger sibling (now in that stage) to join in. Of course, it's five years later now.

What's going on here?

It's normal for kids in the preteens and early teens to have social anxiety. Girls that were social butterflies last year suddenly turn back into caterpillars, in search of a cocoon somewhere. Boys who never met a stranger now react to social events like they're punishments. When the family is getting ready to leave for a gathering, it's frustrating to have a sudden meltdown on your hands.

Should we just expect it, though?

Probably so. Consider just the physical changes underway in both sexes. They're growing fast, and suddenly their limbs are out of proportion, clothes no longer fit, and klutziness is the rule of the day. Hands and feet don't always work like they should. A downy mustache or the hint of a figure may have appeared, and the young person may be torn between fear that someone will notice and fear that they might *not*. Seeing other young people in the same state of change may embarrass them or provoke curiosity and comparison.

Intellectually, their new ability to analyze ideas and to think about perspectives other than their own means that they tend to overthink things, jump to the wrong conclusions, and deliver outrageously inaccurate pronouncements from their limited experience and understanding. In short, they tend to say things they regret.

Emotionally, they are riding a rollercoaster with no seatbelts. They're thrown from anger to depression in a heartbeat. They usually don't understand the hormonal cause of their feelings and just take them at face value instead. This means they overreact and over-emote to normal situations.

Spiritually, they're often struggling with doubts. They find it hard to believe that they have worth simply because God made them and loves them.

And in the midst of all this, they're struggling between wanting to be adults and never wanting to grow up. It's a perfect storm, socially.

Social avoidance

One of the most common ways preteens cope is by avoidance. They just don't want to go anywhere or do anything. Sometimes they'll rebel at going to an event they've attended every week for years. They feel unbearably awkward and will do anything to avoid situations where they think they might be embarrassed.

So, how do you handle it? Generally, you should make them go anyway. Moods often swing quickly, and once they arrive at the event, the resistance they displayed at home may have dissipated already, or the sight of friends or the activity itself may distract them from their previous ill temper. A good experience this time might encourage them for the next opportunity.

However, good influences at the point of arrival don't get your young person in the car to begin with. What's to be done at the start?

Remember to be the calm, stable, *adult* voice in the conversation. *They* sure aren't. Some understanding coupled with direction can help. "I know you feel awkward about this. That's normal at your age. I remember feeling the same way. It's important that we do this today, though, so why don't you go wash your face and get your shoes on. We'll be leaving in about 15 minutes." Often they'll calm down once the decision has been made and they're busy getting ready.

Sometimes, though, your preteen may become so distraught that waiting for them to calm down may destroy the event for everyone else. On rare occasions, we've relented and not required one to attend a given event—but very, very rarely. There are two cautions in this case. On the one hand, you will need to follow up afterward with any correction or consequences for the outburst; you never want to leave the impression that tantrums get results, and an emotional storm of this magnitude may qualify as a tantrum. You also need to be careful that your child is not depressed and distraught beyond "normal" preteen drama. They aren't thinking clearly at this point, and if there's any chance they might harm themselves, obviously you shouldn't leave them alone—and you should look for serious help afterward.[1]

We don't budge if the issue is church. The Word tells us we should not be *forsaking the assembling of ourselves together,*[2] and we should not start a pattern of skipping out on the gathering of our spiritual family. Besides, it makes no sense for someone struggling with their emotions and spiritual life to avoid church—that's where we hear the Bible preached, get accountability, and enjoy the love and encouragement of other Christians. Sorry, kiddo, you're going with us.

---

[1] In certain situations, too, a preteen may simply be too young to be left totally alone, which makes the whole situation more acute for everybody.

[2] Hebrews 10:25

Bullying and being bullied

Our sons played football for several years, and the youth division—basically, the middle schoolers—was the most mismatched assortment in the whole program. Puberty can start any time between 8 and 16, so boys on the same team, the same exact age, might range 12 inches and 100 pounds from each other. It becomes blindingly obvious whenever kids are grouped by grade level or birth years, and those who develop early and whose who develop late can both be rich targets for ridicule and bullying.

It's a prime time for bullies to make their appearance anyway, with all the uncertainty and insecurity in kids' hearts and minds during this state. And it can be a devastating experience for a child who's already struggling with unfamiliar emotions to be singled out for mockery or snubbing.

What's frustrating is that often it's invisible to adults. Mean kids seem to have a talent for ingratiating grown-ups while being incredibly hateful toward other kids; that's why being a "teacher's pet" got such a bad name in school. A friend of ours was bullied for years by the other youth in her church without her parents ever realizing it. Since children of church leaders were involved, she was afraid to tell. It's been very hard for her to overcome, even as a successful adult.

We need to talk to our kids about their relationship with friends and listen for hints that something isn't right. If you find out your child is being bullied, you the parent will need to deal with it.

That doesn't mean that Mama automatically picks up the phone. One option is to teach kids how to stand up to bullies. Many bullies seek out victims they perceive as vulnerable because they are secretly cowards themselves; their cruelty toward another child may be partly to deflect attention away from themselves. Often it means the good kids, the ones who try to avoid trouble and don't pick fights, are the ones who get picked on. However, if a child stands up to them, often bullies will back down—they weren't looking for resistance when they chose their target! When it's physical intimidation (common among boys but not unknown among girls), it's important to tell our children not to *start* a fight, but if someone else starts it, they definitely can and probably should defend themselves.

At this point, some believers will object on the grounds of Jesus' words about "turning the other cheek."[3] It's true that we should be training our children to be peacemakers and to avoid trouble wherever possible; they should not resort to fighting over taunting words, for instance, and if they can overlook an offense, it is a credit to them.[4] However, we don't believe this passage requires a child to submit to a playground beating by an older or larger bully. Assault is an entirely different matter than mere insult, self-defense is not the same thing as revenge and retaliation, and we believe they are entirely within their Biblical rights to defend themselves against a physical attack until help and protection arrives.[5]

Words do hurt

I t may be harder for our kids to understand and respond to verbal bullying than the physical kind, and yet, don't many of us face unwelcome teasing as adults, even? How do *you* respond to a co-worker or neighborhood busybody who makes light of your family choices (large family, small family, homeschooling, adoption), political leanings (as deduced from your bumper stickers or yard signs), or other visible distinctions that surround you? You've learned how to laugh with some comments, to ignore some, to send a smart remark back over the net, or sometimes engage with a serious reply—

---

[3] Matthew 5:38-42
[4] Proverbs 19:11
[5] We're aware this opens a larger debate about Christian pacifism and non-violence.

because different situations may call for different replies. Knowing how to handle a verbal jibe is a good social skill even when it doesn't sink to the level of abuse and intimidation.

If your child is getting picked on, he or she can tell you quite specifically what their tormentors focus on. Their frustration, beyond the pain and embarrassment, is probably what the French call, *l'espirit d'escalier*—"staircase wit."[6] It amounts to an inability to make an effective response until the time has passed. Here's where role-playing can help; by gently talking through the bullying with your child, you can lead him or her into a discussion of more satisfactory ways to respond verbally.

There may be some situations where your presence as a watchful parent can deter the bullying behavior. If it's an incidental thing which happens on the playground after a certain event, for example, you might make yourself visible and keep an unobtrusive eye on things. Bullies don't flourish under supervision.

This won't be possible in every circumstance, though. Things happen behind the doors of school or deep on a playing field, and parents just can't be everywhere. In some cases, a parent appearing on the scene may simply drive the bullying indoors with the additional jabs of "running to Mama" rather than the child standing up for himself.

Ultimately, if standing up to the bully doesn't work, and appealing to the adults in charge is not resolving the problem, and it's impossible for your child to laugh it off or "rise above it," you will need to think about removing your child from the situation. Bullying at this stage, when a child is already uncertain and uncomfortable with herself,

---

[6] The French philosopher Denis Diderot explained that he once was confronted by an outrageous comment at dinner, and wrote that, "a sensitive man, such as myself, overwhelmed by the argument levelled against him, becomes confused and can only think clearly again [when he reaches] the bottom of the stairs"—in other words, on the way out the door. For more discussion, see "L'esprit De L'escalier." *Wikipedia*. Wikimedia Foundation, n.d. Web. 03 Sept. 2016.

can be crippling for life. It may well be that your child needs to be in a different school or even a different church, as difficult as that may be. It's worth doing what it takes.

What if your own child is the bully?

t is entirely possible, of course, that you find yourself on the other side of the problem. What if your preteen has become a bully toward other children?

Sadly, the outworking of original sin in all of us can lead into this role. New feelings of size and strength, or a self-perception that he is more clever than his younger sibling, might tempt an otherwise agreeable child to use their abilities against another. Often this age is a time when young people try on different styles of self-expression, and becoming a "mean girl" or a "tough guy" may be an option they consider.

So if your child is heading in this direction—or may have started a pattern of cruelty to others already—you may be seeing signs of it at home. You notice they're constantly provoking siblings to tears or perhaps you overhear them taunting the younger children. Take no prisoners, Mom and Dad! This needs to be stopped *now*, not only for the sake of their brothers and sisters, but for their own. We know adults whose bullying at home alienated their siblings as children, and they would give almost anything to restore those broken relationships now.

A weird combination

ids this age are a strange mix of adult and child in many ways. We've always been amazed to see young women in their early teens dressed for a formal school presentation, handling themselves with grace and confidence far beyond their years—then jumping and squealing a five-year-olds when when they're announced as winners in the competition.

In social situations, they can be both perceptive and clueless at the same time. Sometimes they show remarkable kindness and insight into other's feelings; frequently, though, they are completely unaware of what they are doing and how that affects others.

Role-playing can help them understand. "I don't think you're aware of how that sounds to the person you are talking to," you might say. "I know you think it's funny they are a little overweight, but I know you're sensitive about being short. I want us to pretend for a moment that *you're* the one being teased at your club meetings. I'm going to pretend to be—let's see, who's a bigger kid you look up to? I know, I'll pretend to be Frank." Then using a different voice, "Hey, short stuff! Are you a hobbit or a dwarf? Oh, I know, you're a little kid! You're not big enough to be in our club. Why don't you go hang around with the other little children!" Then changing your voice back, "How do you think that would make you feel?"

Does that sound harsh? Maybe, but your purpose is to help them perceive the other person's point of view. In their self-centered minds, they often forget that other people have needs and feelings just as valid as their own. They need to know that cruel teasing is displeasing to God; the Bible tells us *be kind to one another, tenderhearted, forgiving one another, even as God in Christ forgave you...*[7] *And just as you want men to do to you, you also do to them likewise.*[8] In fact, you might point out to them the Bible specifically warns against teasing people over physical limitations or disabilities—prime targets for young bullies.[9]

---

[7] Ephesians 4:32

[8] Luke 6:31

[9] *"You shall not curse the deaf, nor put a stumbling block before the blind, but shall fear your God: I am the LORD."* Leviticus 19:14

It's mortifying to realize that *your* child is the queen bee, bully, or thug. You may have thought that "bad kids" must come from bad homes, where they learn awful behavior from awful parents. Certainly, that is true in some cases, and yet we've noticed that the parents of these kids are often super-polite, gentle people—it seems the worst kids (in the eyes of other children) have the nicest parents. Maybe you can't imagine that *your* child would ever behave that way... but if someone *does* approach you with a complaint, it might pay to listen to them and ask the question. Watch for signs of mean behavior or selfishness that tends toward cruelty. A bully left to himself has a bleak future, and it's a lifestyle best dealt with while they're young and the effects are still manageable.

General gormlessness

Our whole family has a love of British things—we enjoy epic TV series from the BBC, our bookshelves are full of British mysteries, P.G. Wodehouse, and biographies of Winston Churchill, and we often quote from *Winnie-the-Pooh* and *All Creatures Great and Small*. Our oldest son spent a year at Oxford and bought a British car nearly as old as he is to tinker with.

Naturally, we picked up some British vocabulary along the way. One of our favorite terms for kids this age is "gormlessness." It comes from a Middle English word meaning "sense", so the lack of "gorm" is basically a mild sort of foolishness or stupidity. They're full of nonsense, goofy, i.e., *gormless*.

To us, it perfectly encapsulates preteen and early-teen humor—odd, weird, silly, ridiculous, coarse, dumb, and often, awkwardly inappropriate for the situation. Have you ever gotten into a pun war with your kids? Dads are often better at this than moms—guys seem to have an appreciation for absurdity. Can you make a rude noise with your armpit or burp on command? You'll be a hit with your preteens.

This sort of comedy can be wildly funny in small doses, but it wears thin pretty fast. Here's the boy who carries himself like a natural born diplomat one moment, then an hour later, collapses in hilarity over passing gas or a joke involving dog droppings. We met a talented girl who could belch the alphabet in reverse, a perfect combination of cleverness and gormlessness rarely encountered.

To make it truly difficult for us as parents and civilizing influences, kids this age are socially tone deaf. Their first steps into adult circles are exhilarating but they can't rely on experience or instinct to guide them, and they may have a hard time guessing what sort of humor is appropriate in public. We've actually told some of our kids at this age, on our way to a public event, "Whatever you do, do *not* try to be funny!" or "Do *not* crack jokes to adults. Do *not* try to get a laugh. Please."

Most kids grow out of this on their own. Others will need coaching. Some will need a *lot* of help.[10] Love them even when they're trying to be funny; relationship is important even when they're making intestinal noises with their hands.

What about social media?

One aspect of relationship-building which is still fairly new on the scene is social media. It's a constantly changing landscape, as the Millennial generation tries out new platforms and stakes out different communities on Facebook, Twitter, Instagram, Snapchat, and the ever-expanding list of options.

---

[10] A book like *The Asperkid's (Secret) Book of Social Rules: The Handbook of Not-So-Obvious Social Guidelines for Tweens and Teens with Asperger's Syndrome* can help kids sort out some of those mysterious social clues—and not just kids with Aspergers! Go to RaisingRealMen.com/preteen-resources/ for a link.

Where does this enter your middle schooler's life? We would suggest, not at all.

When our kids reach the middle-teen years, we *insist* that they start learning social media—not just the platforms, but the etiquette and the dangers of this Wild West community. It's important to help them learn what to share, how much, and where to be more private or selective. Their life online has an impact on college scholarships, job interviews, reputation in the community, and eventually their relationship with a future mate!

And that's a major reason to withhold this very powerful tool from our younger, frankly unstable children in the preteen years.

What's more, raising a profile on social media can make our children into targets for predators and cyberbullying. One of the great tragedies of this era is the way schoolyard tormentors now follow their victims home and continually poison their lives through their social media accounts. This will be a possibility no matter what age our kids are when they go online—it happens to college students and grown up adults, too, sometimes—but our preteens are uniquely vulnerable and impressionable. That also makes them a mark for the growing number of predators online, whose perversion driven by the easy availability of internet pornography.[11] The risk is too great.

So even if their young friends are already online—and we know they are, because some of them became our "friends" on Facebook even after their parents informed us "Our family isn't going to 'do' Facebook"—even so, we've told our kids the time will come soon, *but not yet.*

---

[11] If you doubt this, we suggest you read some of the articles we have on our website, RaisingRealMen.com, as well as the rising statistics of criminal prosecution for child pornography and exploitation the past two decades.

The guy-girl issue

Speaking of *not yet*, there's the shining question of guys and girls and their friendship. Chances are, when you considered this chapter would deal with social awkwardness, you immediately pictured the most awkward society of all—the opposite sex at their own age of uncertainty.

The hormones that change them from children into young men or women also awaken them to the attractions of the opposite sex. It's as if the cooties died like mosquitos in the first frost. Suddenly they look at their playmate or buddy and boys notice, "Wait a minute—she's a girl!" or girls think "Suddenly I feel a little self-conscious around him."

There's a bunch of ways this awakening can play out, from pestering the opposite sex to getting involved in internet porn or dangerous flirtatiousness.

If you haven't already given your kids a solid Biblical attitude toward sexuality, now is the time. Don't think, "My children don't even know sex exists—we control all the entertainment that comes into our home!" Kids are curious and they *will* talk about these things together, so you can assume your ten—or twelve-year-old has already thought about this more than you'd expect. One author we read said if you're reading through the Bible in family devotions, by the time you finish Deuteronomy you've already run into most of this topic!

You also need to get accountability software on every single internet-capable device in your home.[12] Talk to them about how to keep themselves safe from predators, too. We talk about how to do these things in another chapter of this book.

---

[12] Click through to our current recommendation at www.RaisingRealMen.com/safety. This may be an affiliate link which blesses our ministry, as well.

Beyond all those serious things, though, there are some other issues we need to talk about. First is our own attitude and accessibility as parents. If we hope to be able to advise our children on questions of love and sex as they move through the teen years and seeking their future spouses, we have to lay the foundations here and guard them carefully. Our primary rule is simple: **Don't freak out.** No matter what the question, our kids need to know and *feel* they can ask Mom or Dad and get a thoughtful answer. Don't be shocked. No matter what they ask, take a deep breath and then answer calmly. Don't scoff or make fun of them—even a little bit of teasing about the opposite sex can clam up a kid for months if not longer (ask us how we know).

In the preteen years, it's pretty normal for kids to have a first crush on someone. Everything in the entertainment industry promotes it, as if the hormonal rush didn't push them toward the opposite sex in a way they never expected anyway. That's why it's a good idea to talk about your family's ideas about finding a mate long before they have a full-fledged infatuation going.

In our family, we encourage our kids to avoid romantic attachments until they're approaching marriageable age—which can be different ages for different kids even in the same family. That is not to suggest they need to have a career and own a house before they start looking for a mate! However, there is really no point in encouraging twelve—and fourteen-year-olds to go head-over-heels in love with someone they won't be able to marry for years and years to come. Why invest all the emotional energy and uproar associated with teen romance, when the likely results will be frustration, hurt feelings, or even inappropriate intimacy, before a permanent relationship is even possible?

This caution doesn't argue for strict separation of the sexes, though. Some families, concerned about the same things we are, go so far as to teach their kids that it is impossible (repeat, *impossible*) for a boy and girl to have a friendship that doesn't drive them toward sex. That's just not so. We simply point to the apostle's directions to young Timothy, his church-planting protégé in Crete—to "*encourage... younger women as sisters, in all purity.*"[13] That sort of relationship is neither fearful, passionate, nor suspicious; it's respectful, friendly, and chaste.

A biblically balanced view of relationships

A great deal has been said and written in Christian circles by teachers advocating the full range of relationship models, from leaving everything to the kids, to parent-arranged unions. We found if you read through the Scriptures, there are examples of just about any arrangement you can imagine involving heterosexual marriages; there does not seem to be a single "correct" model for finding a mate "God's way." Instead, we see several principles that we teach our kids early in the process:

1. **All relationships must be honoring to God** –...*whatever you do, do all to the glory of God.*[14]

2. **Christians should only marry other Christians**— *Do not be unequally yoked together with unbelievers, for what fellowship has righteousness with darkness?*[15]

3. **Be intentional**, and don't start a romantic relationship you can't or shouldn't complete –... *no one should take advantage of and defraud his brother in this matter [of sexual purity]...*[16]

---

[13] 1 Timothy 5:1-2 (ESV)
[14] 1 Corinthians 10:31b
[15] 2 Corinthians 6:14
[16] 1 Thessalonians 4:6

4. **Don't go off into sexual immorality**—*For this you know, that no fornicator... has any inheritance in the Kingdom of God.*[17]

5. **Don't forget to** *Honor your father and your mother, which is the first commandment with a promise.*[18]

Beyond these basic commandment-level Scriptures, there seems to be an immensely wide range of alternatives for finding and winning a mate... Biblically speaking. Many of them won't apply in our modern times (we wouldn't recommend sending an employee to select a mate for your son from kinfolk several days away, for instance[19]), but our point would be to make certain of the principles, then discuss and advise on the details as they arise.

And culture does make a difference. In our country and society, it's hard for a young couple to support themselves if they haven't finished high school, for example, even though it may be technically *legal* to be married younger. What's more, there is a lot of growing up and maturing that happens between middle school and age 18, isn't there? People are changing, and your child will probably find himself—and the girl who has fascinated him—different in a few years.

It's important to remember the old folk wisdom, "It may be 'puppy love,' but it feels like love to the puppy." If your child expresses a crush or an interest, take her seriously. Talk about God's purpose for marriage, and the feelings which attract us to our mates, and then the wisdom of waiting a few more years before exploring that area. Encourage her to focus on being a friend-who-is-a-girl, rather than a

---

[17] Ephesians 5:5—though it should always be remembered Paul's similar words to the Corinthians reminded them that "*such were some of you. But you were washed, but you were sanctified, but you were justified in the name of the Lord Jesus and by the Spirit of our God.*" 1 Corinthians 6:9-11

[18] Ephesians 6:2

[19] That's how Isaac and Rebekah were introduced, in Genesis 24

girlfriend. You might say, "I understand. He is definitely a nice boy. It's going to be years, though, before you're ready to get married, so I suggest you just put all that aside and be friends. In a few years, you'll be better able to tell what kind of man he's turning out to be."

The unfortunate reverse psychology of boys

Just as a boy with sudden physical changes will become clumsy and accident-prone, a boy who finds himself suddenly drawn toward a girl he's known as a classmate or neighborhood friend may become just as awkward in the emotional-romantic sense. In the throes of a crush, he may not know what to do with himself, but in a weird attempt to gain the girl's attention, start pestering or teasing the object of his new affection.

Does this make sense? No, but it happens. Your son, poor soul, needs to be reminded that no one likes being tormented. If he wants to show the girl his admiration, he needs to be polite and considerate to her. At the same time, though, he needs the same message you might give your daughter at this age—that it's better to wait on romance for a few more years, and instead, become a gentleman and a friend-who-happens-to-be-a-boy for now. The time will come soon enough!

On the other hand, if your daughter is the recipient of this sort of attention, it's not a good idea to tell her, "Oh, honey, that means he likes you! You should play along and enjoy the attention." Would you say the same thing if she were seventeen, and her nineteen-year-old boyfriend showed his affection by roughing her up a little? We don't want our daughters to ever think it's acceptable for a man to express his attention in unpleasant or uncomfortable ways. Instead, we say, "Sometimes boys express themselves in really foolish ways. He may like you, but it's not okay for him to do things that make you feel uncomfortable or unsafe. Just tell him, 'No!'"

Now is the foundation for good things ahead

We found with our house cats first, and then with our babies, that if you establish expectations and traditions early on, there is less struggle over them later. Starting the conversations about love, marriage, and sexuality when your kids are preteens (and even earlier) can smooth the way for deeper discussions when they're teenagers and beyond.

Your middle schooler may die of embarrassment when you start one of these conversations. Sometimes they blush and plead, "Awkward, Mom! *Puh-leeeze*, can we talk about something else?" but if the time seems appropriate, we just press on![20] It's important that we do this so they have their parents' advice and a Biblical view of relationships to build upon.

It's also important that we give them hope... and at the right time, "permission!" After all, we may tell our eleven-year-old, "Don't go looking at the girls and wondering 'Would that one make a good wife?'", but he needs to know that when he's twenty-one, yes, he probably *ought* to be looking at the girls and asking that question! Several of our twenty-something friends told us that their parents were so worried about any kind of male-female interaction, even friendship, that once the time was right to think about finding a mate and getting married, they felt guilty about talking to the opposite sex—even in the godliest, most intentional way. That's sad.

We try to explain to our young people from a very young age that Christian marriage is *wonderful*. We tell them how much we love each other and how much we've enjoyed being married. We tell them our love story. We tell them we're praying for the young people

---

[20] If they are really, really sheepish about these talks, we suggest bringing it up in the car late at night sometimes—when you're both looking through the windshield, and nobody can see anyone blush.

that will marry our children one day. Since most young people will eventually marry, we want them to look forward to it.

He who finds a wife finds a good thing,
And obtains favor from the Lord.[21]

And we all look forward to the end of all this social awkwardness. This, too, will pass!

---

[21] Proverbs 18:22

Media, Gaming, And Discernment

7

Once upon a time, in the early years of the 20th century, a father somewhere probably looked around the kitchen table at his expectantly-waiting teenagers and said, "Children, I have heard your pleas and I have prayed over your request, but honestly, I can't see it. We are *not* going to install a telephone in this home; it will only encourage idle gossip."

Of course, Dad would have been right. The telephone did bring new ways to waste time and certainly facilitated gossip like never before. Yet at the same time, it rapidly became an indispensable tool for connecting a family to the community—to the neighbors (who often shared the same phone line!), to the grocer, to the doctor when he was needed. And a generation later, a person who wasn't "on the phone" or "in the book" was finding himself increasingly isolated.

The Internet in all its manifestations has become the new "required" communication tool. We've seen the same evolution of intention and result in our generation. We have friends who said, "I see enough email at work, I don't want it at home," or declared, "The Internet is full of traps and sin, and there's nothing my kids need to access," or maybe, "Facebook is just a bulletin board for stupid pictures of cats who can't spell and snapshots of folks' breakfast; what a waste of time!"

Like our hypothetical ancestor's view of Alexander Graham Bell's wonderful invention, all of the above is partially true. A lot of us are ready to turn off the email hydrant when we have permission from our boss. Social media does serve up a lot of drivel and nonsense. And the Internet might best be seen as the gateway to a huge, mostly unregulated city—complete with art museums and gambling halls, libraries and dens of all kinds of iniquity.

But we've watched as our friends, who resolved to go offline at home, faded out from many of our community activities. They simply weren't getting the messages and announcements any more, once the local groups stopped mailing printed newsletters and the newspaper stopped carrying local news. The current generation of young adults relies on social media as the first step to befriending one another -if you're not on social media, you basically don't exist.

So what else is new?

We have friends who grew up in the Amish faith, and others who live and work near Amish, Mennonite, and German Baptist Brethren settlements in Pennsylvania, Ohio, and Missouri. Surely these are the communities where the digital revolution means little or nothing. Yet we hear from those close to them that even in these ultra-conservative settlements, islands of connectivity have quietly moved in; after all, Amish farmers and craftsmen have customers and suppliers beyond their church circles, and most outsiders prefer an email to a postcard now.

Few of us are preparing our kids for radically agrarian lifestyles or a post-apocalyptic world. Very soon they'll be expected to understand and use technology for communication, and in most cases, they'll be like us—looking at a screen for much of the business day, and then relaxing with an e-book or on-demand entertainment channeled through the same devices. The questions for the parent of a preteen are something along the lines of "Now?" and "How much?"

What is changing, and what is not

One thing we've learned over the years is that directions and methods we followed for raising our three-year-old weren't the most effective when they were thirteen, and were *totally* inappropriate for advising our twenty-three-year-old!

Putting that into practice is not as obvious as it seems. We often struggle with notions of "fairness" and "equal treatment" which really don't apply at home. Our older kids will quickly remind us, "You never let *us* do that!" or the younger ones will demand to know why big sister is allowed to be on Facebook but little sister isn't. It is perfectly appropriate to tell a younger child, "You're not old enough," or, "Your eighteen-year-old brother has different rules *and* different responsibilities than you do." Don't be cowed by protest movements at home!

But preparing our kids for their digitized future is going to involve training them to use devices and media with wisdom, discernment, and a healthy level of skepticism. Our own parents wrestled over what role television would play in family life. Our generation has found that the newest media prompts the same questions.

One of the most common is, "What do you do about 'screen time'?" Many parents are uneasy about their family's media habits; they have a feeling things are out of control and they don't know what to do about it—if there's any hope of changing habits at all. On the other hand, we've met families who've completely banished any sort of media or electronics from their kids' lives... but don't seem to know when their children *do* need to start using computers and engaging the media culture.

The frustration and concern is understandable. There's a lot of waste and temptation "out there." None of us want to raise our children as passive viewers or compulsive gamers. Yet outside those communities, our kids will be expected to have access to the net and know how to use it. If we don't prepare them at home, they won't be ready for modern adulthood.

A time of transition

D octors and counselors advise parents that small children need very limited time as passive viewers. The advice hasn't changed from the introduction of black and white TVs to the era of binge-watching movies on your smart phone. Young kids benefit much more from active play, imagination, and exploration, than from watching even "good" programs on the screen.

But, what about preteens. What then?

From protected to guided

I n our sunny south, the winters are short and the growing season is long. Our friends in colder climates have to start their tender plants in cold frames or greenhouses to make the most of the shorter summer, protecting the shoots and sprouts from the last killing frosts of winter. And if those young tomato plants are going to survive outside the greenhouse, they'll need to be hardened off, carefully exposed to the weather and sunlight day by day until they are strong enough to stand on their own outside.

It's the same with our children. Like the young plants in the greenhouse, we want to protect our young children from exposure to things that may tempt or harm them. We shield them from serious media violence, disturbing story themes, "adult" situations. We don't want the media our kids see to be mixed in any way.

The problem is that by the time they are adults they will need to be able to discern good and bad media for themselves. We've got to teach them how to do that. We have to teach them discernment.

> *But solid food belongs to those who are of full age, that is, those who by reason of use have their senses exercised to discern both good and evil.*[1]

The preteens and early teens are a good time to teach our kids how to watch media through a Biblical lens, analyzing and interpreting the messages they receive. That means you gradually begin to watch some things that have a few issues and teach your children how to identify the problems and examine them in the light of God's Word.

The power of art

The Christian philosopher Francis Schaeffer made a crucial point in his short but powerful book, *Art and the Bible*. Whenever we consider at a creative work—whether it's a painting, a sculpture, a dance performance, or a television program—we are looking at two things. First, there is the skill of the artist. Can he draw well? Does she dance with grace? Did the director grip your attention and emotion during the film?

But underneath the artistic technique, there's the critically important matter of the message. The paint, musical notes, and computer-generated effects are simply the way ideas are communicated, just like pixels on screen or ink on paper. We need to ask ourselves, and teach our kids to ask, "What are they telling me here? Is it true? Is it good?"

We've probably all had the experience of humming along to a tune we remember from high school or college, and suddenly realizing the words are not appropriate to share with our six-year-old sitting

---

[1] Hebrews 5:14

next to us. We stumbled into the trap of good art—a catchy tune, an exciting movie, a likeable character—that was communicating a bad message.

This is a great concept to emphasize with your young people. No one will try to lead them astray or defraud them with an unattractive presentation. A hunter baits his traps with the thing his quarry really likes. So we should coach our preteens and teens to avoid those traps by always asking, "What's the message? What does the artist want me to feel, think, and respond to? And is it right?"

Teach them to recognize good art, but always seek out good art which is communicating a good message—and reject it, if it's not!

What's the theme?

One of the first things to teach your children is to identify the theme of what they are watching. The theme is more than the plot or story—it's the overarching message the writer or direction is trying to communicate to you.

One of our family's favorite movies is the Pixar animated feature, *The Incredibles.* If you ask your young preteen to describe the film, he's likely to say, "It's about a superhero family who has to live undercover." But that's actually the subject or topic. The theme is the answer to the question, "What does the moviemaker want you to think or believe from this film?"

Often there is more than one theme. In *The Incredibles,* the major theme is "Be content with the gifts you've been given and fulfill your own mission in life." There is constant trouble for the family who must hide their superhuman abilities while the world needs their help—while the villain, unhappy that he's not "super," uses his remarkable intelligence for revenge rather than virtue. Another theme is that marriage and family are critical to fulfilling that mission. Although *The Incredibles* is not a Christian movie per se, the basic themes are very compatible with a Christian worldview.

Sometimes entertainment which seems benign may actually carry a very negative theme. The animated version of Dr. Seuss' *The Lorax* looks like a harmless cartoon based on the picture book by a trusted children's author. However, themes emphasized in the film send a powerful message that small, family-owned businesses are evil and dangerous for the planet. The Lorax himself is set up as a savior-figure focused on plants, not people; there is even an ascension and a second-coming scene, if you missed the parallel to Jesus. We don't want our small children confused about the Lord and suspicious of all business life, so we wouldn't show this to a young child at all. On the other hand, it can be an excellent lesson in themes and messaging to watch and discuss with a preteen or teen.

Character matters

Another area of media discernment is characterization. How are the people who carry out the story portrayed? Are we invited to identify with them in some way? Is our sympathy drawn toward certain characters? And critically, should we identify and sympathize with the character as portrayed?

One summer during our annual trip to "the lake," Melanie started reading a novel a previous guest had left behind. It was well-written and Melanie could hardly avoid cheering for the winsome young woman in the story—until she realized the woman's goal was to commit adultery. Should we cheer for this? She threw it out.

Hal had a similar experience reading Agatha Christie's classic *The Murder of Roger Ackroyd*. The novel is written with a first-person narrator which naturally draws the reader to identify with him. Through the narrator's eyes, the reader watches the great detective unravel the crime. Imagine the horror when the conclusion reveals that the reader's alter ego, the narrator himself, is the killer! Hal said it made him feel somehow defiled (and quite displeased with Christie's trick).

There is a place for the portrayal of evil. We live in a sinful world, and the best stories recognize the great story of sin, sacrifice, and redemption. Many stories follow the reformation of a character who starts off as selfish, complacent, or dissipated, but through the events of the story, are changed to become better persons in the end. Others set up a clear narrative of good and evil, where sin bears its fruit in the lives of the characters and justice prevails even through difficulties.

But it is important to make a distinction about stories which celebrate moral inversion. Is the hero an unrepentant thief, a vigilante, a seducer, or con artist? Is the story meant to glorify a successful robbery caper, an illicit love affair, or false spirituality?

On the other side, are characters who are called to higher standards portrayed as bad guys? We are commanded to be in submission to certain authorities—parents, pastors, lawmakers and magistrates, and so forth. Do people in these roles sometimes abuse them and fail to live up to their righteous calling? Certainly they do, and it is legitimate to tell stories about corrupt politicians and hypocritical preachers. But are they understood as exceptions, and do they experience redemption or justice in the course of the story? Or does the story send the message that leaders are naturally suspect and that disobedience or rebellion are acts of heroism?

God says through the prophet Isaiah, *"Woe to those who call evil good, and good evil; who put darkness for light, and light for darkness; who put bitter for sweet, and sweet for bitter!"*[2] The proverbs warn that it is

---

[2] Isaiah 5:20

foolishness to make light of sin, and even unrighteous rulers and compromised religious leaders should receive a measure of respect for the position, even if the individual is unworthy of his title.[3]

Genres

We humans naturally classify things. It helps us when we can put ideas into categories, and then think about them as a group rather than a million individual problems. Stories are an example of this; there are certain genres that have common characteristics, and it's a good topic to discuss with your young people.

For example, what are common themes in the classic Westerns? They tend to be stories about law and order. There are good guys and bad guys, there are disputed claims and simmering feuds, and usually justice comes about at the end. The idea that there is a moral law that must be upheld and victorious at the finish is a good, Biblical principle. However, many of these stories try to establish order by vigilante law. Often the story involves a character who takes the law into his own hands, and there is a hunt for revenge rather than due process; "You shot my Pa, now you're gonna die." This is where they run off the trail. "*Beloved,*" wrote the apostle, "*do not avenge yourselves, but rather give place to wrath; for it is written, 'Vengeance is Mine, I will repay,' says the Lord.*"[4] The proper response is to bring the wicked to justice—the established justice of the magistrate, "*for he does not bear the sword in vain; for he is God's minister, an avenger to execute wrath on him who practices evil.*"[5]

---

[3] "Fools mock at sin, But among the upright *there is* favor.," Proverbs 14:9. It is worthwhile to notice that the apostle Paul apologized for speaking sharply of the unrighteous high priest (Acts 23:5) and told the early Christians to honor their earthly rulers—even in the context of pagan Rome, where the emperor was worshiped as a god. (Romans 13:1)

[4] Romans 12:19, quoting Deuteronomy 32:35

[5] Romans 13:4

This theme also shows up in other adventure stories, like some police dramas and even the old Robin Hood sagas—to steal from the rich is still stealing, even if the stolen goods are used to help the poor.

Science fiction and fantasy are immensely popular among young people; they seem generationally eager to look ahead to a future full of amazing possibilities. The idea of harnessing undiscovered new technologies and sources of power borders on magical. Naturally, it's exciting!

Sometimes the futuristic setting is used to re-tell unchanging human stories—Gene Roddenberry, the creator of *Star Trek*, famously sold studio executives on the concept of "*Wagon Train* to the stars," comparing it to a popular TV Western series. Many of the older episodes could have been set along the ancient Silk Road, on the decks of a Columbus' galleons, or aboard a World War II destroyer without major modification to the story.

But here is the caution of these genres—often, they take advantage of the idea of new and unfamiliar settings to suggest that God's law doesn't extend to these parts of the universe. Sometimes the writers set personal autonomy as the highest virtue, and individual will and desire as the measure of good or evil. Frequently the hero is simply amoral—living by his own personal code—or ironically, the source of power and wisdom is connected to a religious proposition, whether the pantheistic and impersonal "Force" of the *Star Wars* saga, or magical totems and spells of Harry Potter.

When a story truly delves into horror, the supernatural, and the occult, there is a serious problem. There truly is an unseen, spiritual world, and there truly are forces and actors which we neither see nor control—and yet have an impact in our physical world. The Scripture tells us the fallen angels and death itself will be defeated at the end, but we still can't play games with them in the present. So much of the tragedy of ancient Israel's history came about when the people looked away from God and asked, "What do these other religions have to offer?" To glorify the forces of spiritual evil or suggest that dark powers are available to willing mortals is treason to our Creator.

Techniques

The artistic technique also communicates. Film is a powerful place to demonstrate this, combining not only the acting and dialogue, but effects of lighting, camera technique, and music to guide the viewer's experience.

The classic black and white film *Casablanca* shows how lighting is a subtle but powerful tool. Whenever the hero, Rick, is on screen, he's in a pool of light. Even if the room is dark, there will be a stripe of light from a window or doorway that illuminates Humphrey Bogart's character. On the other hand, the villains of the story tend to be in the shadows. The effect is low key, but if you notice, it's there.

The Wizard of Oz starts out in black and white, like most of the movies of that time. Dorothy's Kansas is mundane, and grows darker as the storms arise. Yet when she awakens in the magical land of Oz, the view is not just in color—it's *unbelievably* colorful. Everything is vivid, even garish—until the adventure ends and she returns to "reality"— her black and white home and family on the prairie. Even though you realize that Kansas in 1939 actually did exist in color—it was just the less expensive film that recorded it in monochrome—you still receive the message that Oz is an infinitely cooler place than the Great Plains.

And where would the films that make up *The Lord of the Rings, Star Wars,* and Indiana Jones epics be without the incredible film scores of Howard Shore and John Williams? Notice how different themes and melodies appear in the background as different characters enter the picture. Listen how Shore uses the wistful, Celtic tunes of the Shire to emphasize the homesickness and isolation of the gentle hobbits, in contrast with the heroic but ominous themes that accompany their journey. Compare how Williams shifts between major and minor keys to heighten the drama of the conflict between good and evil forces. Even though we recognize the major theme music of these blockbusters (and their soundtracks quickly acquire a life of their own), the real power lies in the mood-setting backgrounds. Listen for it, and point it out!

Discussion

As you begin to allow your preteens and young teens to watch things that aren't one hundred percent G-rated, you need to increase the time you spend talking with them about the media they're consuming. Whenever we watch a movie at our house, we have a lively discussion afterward. We talk about the theme, characterization, worldview, and how the director and actors carried those ideas out in the film.

You want to show them the inside of the magic hat. When you first see a magician, you're amazed at what he does, but once you know how the tricks are done, you are never entirely able to suspend disbelief again. Once you show your children how writers, composers, and filmmakers are able to manipulate their audience into accepting ideas they wouldn't otherwise, then they are much less susceptible to that manipulation. That's the goal: teach them to analyze media through the lens of God's Word and a Christian worldview.

Gaming

Gaming is often mentioned in the same discussion as other entertainment media, but there are distinctions. Just like books, movies, and music, the issues of worldview, characterization, and theme apply to games, too. The difference with gaming is that the player becomes an actor in the story—not just an observer.

The Word tells us, as we've mentioned before, that the Lord expects more than just outward obedience. The Lord cares about our hearts. When it comes to sin, it doesn't have to be in real life to be sin; unrighteous anger is murder in the spirit, self-indulging lust is adultery in the heart, and so on. If God is weighing the thoughts and intentions of our heart as well as our actions—and He is—then we need to be careful of the fantasy life we let our children pursue.

Obviously there is a full range of games available. A great number of them present no concern at all, other than a temptation to waste time (though that is not a trivial problem, to be sure). Other games reward points to the player who is most successful stealing cars, torturing competitors, and abusing prostitutes. The winning player has wrapped up his conscience with acts of spiritual theft, viciousness, and lust. Is this pleasing to God? Is it something we want to facilitate or permit in the lives of our kids? Of course not.

Gaming is more than simply racing the clock with an inanimate opponent. From the earliest days of computer networking, programmers realized the fun of entering a virtual world with other live players, often gathering from around the globe. Gaming has become a community activity that rivals social media for many players. Relationships are forged as the players encounter and overcome dangers together in their imaginary identities. Actual friendships can develop, and that can be a good thing—or a very bad one.

Recently, a young gamer in Britain was groomed through a friendship he developed online with another, slightly older gamer. After long interaction in the context of the game, the older player invited the younger to visit him to discuss the possibility of working in the programming field. When the younger player traveled to his home, his "friend" took him prisoner, sodomized him, and then killed him.

There's not a straight line from the home video console to a police morgue. The illustration is simply to point out that our young people will need guidance and supervision to keep them out of dangerous territory online. They need to understand that just as they can pretend to be a medieval wizard in an online game, the friend they meet in the chat room may not be a cute 16-year-old redhead but a balding 55-year-old guy sitting in his basement. They need to understand the personal information that needs to stay private, including not just their street address and phone number, but their siblings' names, their favorite after-school hangout, or their church. Predators are real and this is one area they hunt for victims.

One final concern about gaming is its potential to be addictive. You can waste time playing mini-games on your phone, certainly, but the complex and highly realistic games on home consoles can be very intense. In real life, battles tend to last a short time, then armies disengage to reposition and resupply. In gaming, your mind can be in constant battle-mode, releasing adrenaline and dopamine, for hours and hours every day. Research shows some gamers average over six hours a day in play![6] Our bodies aren't meant to handle that kind of hormonal release, hour after hour. Just as we talked about with porn, the receptors begin to shut down, and the person has to play longer and harder for the same thrill. Before long, he's addicted, physically.

That's one reason parents get push back when they try to limit their kids' gaming. Their bodies and brains are craving it! That's also a good reason to limit gaming. Although it is probably a good idea for

---

[6]   The Nielsen Company, "Multi-Platform Gaming: For The Win!" Newswire, 5/27/14. (http://www.nielsen.com/us/en/newswire/2014/multi-platform-gaming-for-the-win.html)

kids to have some experience with video games, so they can have some shared experiences with their peers, for their sakes you have to keep it under control.

One thing that's worked well in our house is to limit access. Melanie's brother is very generous to our children and has bought them several gaming systems. Those stay at their grandmother's house, which works perfectly. They are able to enjoy them there, which makes them want to visit more and keeps them entertained while they're there, but they aren't tempted by them all day. Of course, once they are teens and have their own laptops, they have more access to games, but hopefully by then they have more maturity and less temptation to obsess over things.

Role-playing games are particularly attractive to kids who are struggling with social anxiety or not fitting in, which most preteens struggle with. In the game world, they can choose who they'll be; they can recreate themselves. The trouble is that the fantasy becomes a lot more enticing than reality. Who wants to go to history club where you trip over your own feet on the way in the door, don't know who to sit with, and will probably stutter if somebody talks to you; the game offers the alternative to stay at home and be a brave and honored knight or a lovely warrior maiden. It's a trap. We're meant to live here, in this reality. Fantasy needs to be kept in the realm of reasonable entertainment.

Stepping Back

What if you've realized that your child is spending too much time watching streaming video, or reading the wrong kind of book, or gaming excessively? Then it's time for you to be the adult. You're going to need to help them moderate their usage and change their habits and it's not likely to be easy or pretty.

Remember, though, that you aren't dealing with a small child anymore. You've got to deal with a preteen or young teen in the throes of emotional meltdowns, depressed feelings, and intellectual changes. You might want to reread the chapter on emotions before you talk to them. It's important to talk through the problem with them and explain your concerns before you announce whatever limitations you plan to introduce. How much better it will be if they come to those conclusions themselves!

Stepping Up

We were visiting with a family we met while traveling, and noticed our teens and their teens seemed to be getting along very well. When we mentioned this family to our older sons in college, as people they might like to know, we were met with a shrug. "They're not on social media," one told us. "They don't really exist."

For the twenty-somethings we've met, a social media presence is a basic life requirement. Many of their generations hesitate to reach out to someone until they've checked their profile on Facebook or other platforms. College professors and administrators alike are using social media to post schedules, announcements, and cancellations. One fast food chain has requested job applicants send a message via Snapchat.

Maybe you've avoided all the controversy about online gaming and media by simply keeping your children offline. That's fine. If they've reached their mid-teens, though, we strongly recommend you start teaching them to use the internet, and particularly social media, with discretion. They need to learn to use the internet like a Christian before they are on their own. While they're at home and under your authority, you can coach them on what to post and what to avoid. You can provide the skeptical eye of a grownup to help them understand the suspicion and deceit of the world beyond their family. And you can take steps to train them to recognize the baited hooks and avoid walking into a trap online.

Part of this involves creating a family culture of accountability. We installed software on all of our family's devices, phones included, and gave Mom and Dad the first account.[7] We established the rule of no secrecy, starting with passwords—every online account gets documented and the passwords saved in a vault program or some other kind of record (this includes the two of us, not just the kids). Sharing the keys to our accounts reminds us that we can't run astray without the possibility of being followed and found out (It's also a great help if you find yourself locked out of an account).

Instead of being isolated, we want our older teens and twenties to be warriors for Christ! We've seen young men and women starting theological discussions online and witnessing to their coworkers and college classmates. We've seen them take a public stand for righteousness that all can see. It's pretty amazing and it's a great use of media.

The online world and the media available really are like a large city, as we said. There are art museums, libraries, government archives, and shopping centers. There is a red light district of casinos, con artists, predators, and filth. And there is a vast and growing marketplace of ideas, and indeed, the very "gates of the city" where news and culture are interchanged. During the tween years, our kids need a great deal of supervision and caution when interacting with the internet and the world it accesses. They won't always be preteens, though. They are growing up fast.

---

[7] You can click through to our current recommendation (this may be an affiliate link which supports our ministry) by going to www.RaisingRealMen.com/safety.

Psalm 127 says that our children are gifts from the Lord, and they *"shall not be ashamed, but shall speak with their enemies in the gate."* That should tell us our sons and daughters, when we've trained them, should know where those gates are located, be able to find their way around them, and recognize their enemies—whom they are ready to confront, unashamed and unafraid!

Conflict At Home   8

hree of our pre-teens were "discussing" how to clean up after dinner. We were in a cabin away from home and the usual chore schedule was all out of whack. By the time the "discussion" was done, one was in tears ("You don't love me!"), another was outraged ("Mom, that's emotional blackmail!"), and the other had taken advantage of the bickering to sneak away to the computer again. And nothing had been cleaned yet.

One of the blessings of a large family is that children born closer together may be able to connect and interact in ways kids in smaller families may not. They grow and change so fast in the early years, a difference of four years rather than two means different schools, different interests and activities, different circles of friends, and different levels of development and maturity. The closer spacing has encouraged our children to form natural bonds of friendship as well as their family ties, and we're thankful for that.

On the other hand, when the children are only separated by a couple of years, you can end up like our family in another way—occasionally, you experience overlap. We enjoyed a few memorable years with a late-bloomer on one side and a precocious adolescent on the other of a "typical" pre-teen sibling. Three hormonal tweens at once.

No matter how many children you have or how far apart the siblings are, this is a maddening, turbulent time for your preteen child and the rest of your family. All the other challenges—changes in their thought processes, emotional instability, insecurity about their bodies, spiritual doubts—come out in their family interactions. To be frank, they might be easier to get along with if they kept their uncertainties and fears to themselves—but they don't. They *can't*.

And really, it's good that they can't keep everything inside. In the spirit of Romans 8:28, we need to recognize that their unconscious self-revelation allows us to counsel and guide them through the transition. Their complete lack of filters allows us to see what is going on in their hearts. Otherwise, it would be tempting and easy to convince ourselves that everything was stable, "all systems nominal" like a successful space launch, if we weren't brought up short by the commotion in the house.

The question for us becomes how *do* we guide and counsel these young people, when their struggled thrashing has stirred up all the water around them? When some days nothing is accomplished but a series of emotional meltdowns and refereed fights? When siblings are in a constant state of alert and continual misunderstanding of each other? When everybody's feelings are raw and bruised, all the time?

One mom we know says the only way to survive it is to keep a bottle of wine in the fridge. That's not our style, but we'll confess the dark chocolate sure takes a hit some days. Melanie's been known to keep a jar of chocolate hazelnut spread in her filing cabinet—with a spoon!

A challenging mix

t's not easy being a tween. The whole internal experience of emotional eruptions, overwhelming insecurity, loss of self-control, uncertainty about your identity...it's a tough ride, and that's if you never get out of your own head. When other people come into view, they are pulled right into the pre-adolescent's orbit. Her normal self-centeredness means she doesn't have a great deal of empathy or thoughtfulness. His lack of impulse control means he blurts out whatever drifts into his head—or worse, jumps into immediate action.

Their universal lack of perspective and their impaired executive function means they just don't think things through.

"Did you think for *one second* what was going to happen?" we ask in exasperation. No, actually, they didn't. They're not good or even very capable of that right now. And as a result, sometimes they get hurt or they offend a family member.

Misunderstandings are so common they seem normal at this age. *Are we even speaking the same language?* we wonder. Concepts like "hunger," "fairness," "ownership," and "permission" seem to have fluid definitions. Their intellectual development gives them a desire to analyze and explain things around them, but their lack of experience leads to them to false conclusions unrooted in reality. Their proclamations are emphatic and often hilariously wrong—but *they* are not amused. They frequently boil up with indignation over a sibling, only to find they completely misunderstood the situation. They think they know the other person's intentions, but often, they don't.

How we see each other

As parents, we look at our pre-teens and shake our heads. *I don't know what's gotten into this kid,* we think. They don't respond when we speak to them, and we don't know if they're deaf or defiant. We give them instructions or place boundaries, and they blow right past them—"I didn't hear you," "I thought you were talking to my sister," "I forgot," "But that's not fair," seem to be their stock answers. We correct them for some mistake or oversight, and they fling accusations instead of apologies. Somehow, our sweet, obedient, happy child has become disrespectful, disobedient, disordered in every way—and if they're unhappy, we might not notice because they're making *us* so upset.

Our kids have taken their own unsettled perceptions and found offense with us, too. They want to be treated as grown up, and they don't see how acting like a temperamental nine-year-old makes a difference. They have a heightened sense of Justice and Fairness and Rightness (by their own standards), and our decisions are weighed in their balance found sadly wanting. They feel a need to express themselves and defend their intentions and grievances, and they are shocked—shocked!—that Mom and Dad aren't immediately receptive. Their frustrations overwhelm them and, boys and girls alike, burst into unexpected tears (often to their own dismay!). Their expanding view of the world and their place in it drives them to say *Stop—let me think whether I can accept this or not.*

It's a recipe for conflict.

To be honest, there are some elements of truth in both these perspectives. A clearly disrespectful response is, well, clearly disrespectful. *Honor your father and your mother* does not have a footnote, *unless they really don't get it and they're like totally unfair.* Suffering from hormonal overload and emotional befuddlement and stress doesn't excuse bad behavior, an unpleasant lesson we all have to learn. Yet it's also true that we parents often *do* make mistakes—maybe the change here is that our little boy feels freedom to call it out now (however undiplomatically he does so). And they *are* growing up—that's the whole point of the onset of puberty. Eventually we have to acknowledge that while, "You'll always be 'my little girl,'" she'll likely be the mother of our grandkids one day.

So, when all our emotions and all our frustrations are running high, how can we build—or rebuild—a loving and workable relationship with our fast-changing offspring?

Cultivating and pruning the parent-child relationship

S o much of our family conflict is fraught with emotion, that's a place to start. As the mature party in the uproar, we parents need to control our own emotions first—not easy for any of us, and harder still for some. Yet it's plain that our tweens are not just sources of emotional energy, they pick it up from others in the room and reflect it back with their own. Few things will make us go from zero to righteous indignation more than a child accusing an innocent parent of being angry at them when they *weren't*. And if you've ever had that situation, you know that your rush of outrage simply confirmed the accusation. We need to adopt a judicial temperament—don't let the preteen's outburst provoke us to reaction. A judge faced with a disrespectful defendant or witness doesn't leap down from the bench and tackle the skunk. He holds the authority in the situation, and it's his right, not theirs, to set the tone in the courtroom. If words and behaviors need correction, he can deal with them in a calm, balanced manner, not matching his outburst against theirs.

Our kids respond better to our counseling if we at least take them seriously. Our child's emotions may be irrational in our opinion— whether giddy or weepy, shy or filled with rage—but internally, the feelings are real to our child. If we recognize that reality from their point of view, maybe we can approach them with mercy instead of irritation. Acknowledge their perception and work with them as your starting point.

If you have an understanding of what's going on in their mind and emotions, you can check your own reactions before handing out discipline. A sweet mother we know asked us what kind of punishment she could use to make her daughter get ready in the morning. "I remind her to go brush her teeth after we finish breakfast, then I find her reading in her room," she explained. "I've reminded her a thousand times, and I know it's disobedience because last year she did it every day on her own." As maddening as that is, it's very likely Mom was ascribing wrong motives to her daughter. With all the brain changes and loss of focus, her daughter was likely easily distracted and probably didn't mean to disobey or disappoint her mother at all.

On the other hand, kids this age often ascribe wrong motives to their parents just as easily as their parents do to them. You may hear your child saying, "You just want to see your friends! You don't care how uncomfortable I am at 4-H!" or be confronted with, "You love my little sister more than you do me. You're always criticizing me!" It's hard *not* to be insulted when they impugn your motives like that. Yet a measured response might be a calm response, "No, I don't love either of you more than the other, but your behavior at the moment *is* a problem." And we can always ask ourselves privately, "*Is* there any truth to that? Could it be that I *am* guilty of this?" Then we can decide whether to repent and apologize, or to correct and instruct!

Wrong motives are easily ascribed in both directions. Both parent and child are frustrated. It's just plain hard. When misunderstanding is happening all over the place, it's more critical than ever to maintain the relationship.

The sibling squabble

f you're dealing with an only child (or the last one at home), then managing the parent-tween relationship may be your magnum opus. If there are brothers and sisters in the picture, though, the work becomes much more "interesting."

The anger and sadness that comes with the hormonal surge, coupled with the lack of perspective, mean that a preteen is very easily offended. They overreact with inappropriate anger or unwarranted tears. They are very black-and-white in their moral judgment, and usually they're wearing the white hat—in their own judgment, anyway. All of this adds up to family conflict, with siblings as well as parents.

Preteens are predisposed to resent their older siblings. They are feeling a new sense of adultness, and they want to be treated as grown-ups rather than children. At the same time, it's hard for family members—and particularly siblings—to recognize this change and honor their wish. The preteen is vexed by the privileges given to his older brother but not himself. He makes himself obnoxious grasping to share his bigger sibling's freedom, friendships, and respect—or undermine them if they're withheld.

Naturally, it never helps when the older sister offers condescending advice to the frustrated tween!

On the other side, the irritable preteen frequently loses her temper with the little sister. If she's put in charge, she becomes a petty dictator. Her annoyance is limitless. Her words are sharp. And the little ones are quick to complain. Ultimately, she wants to distance herself from the younger set—after all, she's trying out for *adult* table this year.

When the preteen becomes a disagreeable companion, the siblings tend to respond in kind. With our large family, we've usually had two in this stage at once, and as many as three, with the other children reacting and egging them on. It can be a time of anger, hurt feelings, and non-stop provocation. And it's not what we pictured for our family, at all!

Building (or restoring) family unity

The psalmist tells us, *Depart from evil and do good; Seek peace and pursue it.*[1] There are going to be days when that peace is just a vision in our homes, no matter what we do, and still, we're called to work in that direction. *So far as it depends on you*, the apostle tells us, *be at peace with all men.*[2] And certainly, we want our children to be at peace with one another!

Every once in a while, we sit down with our kids and remind them they are important to each other. We don't want to be maudlin about it, but it's certain that one day we parents will be with the Lord and the only people who will share the children's memories, the only ones who remember the fun and the exciting and even the sad and frightening times we had will be themselves. If they don't protect and nurture their relationship, where will that leave them?

We had a good friend who freely admitted that, as the older sister in her large family, she was *mean*. She had a cruel sense of humor and a barbed tongue, and she made her younger siblings miserable growing up. Then in college, she met her Lord and Savior, and everything changed. She repented of her wretched behavior and went to her brothers and sisters to seek their forgiveness. To her dismay, there was no forgiveness to offer. Not only was her apology rejected, her siblings weren't interested to hear about her new relationship with Jesus. Years later, one sister—and only one—had come to the Lord herself, and that was her only healthy connection with her large group of siblings. Like the foolish woman in the Proverbs, she had destroyed her relationships with her own hands.[3]

---

[1] Psalm 34:14 and 1 Peter 3:11

[2] Romans 12:18 (NASB)

[3] *The wise woman builds her house, but the foolish tears it down with her own hands.* Proverbs 14:1 (NASB)

We also need to remind them that real love means putting another's needs ahead of your own. You may be delighted with the opportunity to make a joke at your sister's expense, maybe you can really put something over on your brother, but the loving response may be to keep that wit to yourself. Don't zing your sibling if they're not in a jovial mood.

And we have an iron-clad rule in our home that we don't mock one another, especially in areas that may be sensitive or hurtful. The Bible tells us that brothers should stand up for one another and normally ought to be closer than outside friendships.[4] We should just *expect* our closest family to be the most reliable and loyal to us—not the ones who spotlight where our skeletons and tripwires are hidden.

To have those good memories for the future, the family needs to build memories together in the present. Friendships are built on shared experiences, and that goes for friendships within the family too. Preteens are right on the doorstep of the busiest years of their young lives, going into high school, and older siblings are already there. If you want to have those bonding experiences with the preteens, and older kids in particular, parents will have to make sure time is set apart for them. Kids' schedules fill up just like parents' do. Even if you're juggling school calendars, sports practice, Scouting events, and dance lessons, you need to make a priority for activities you can share as a family, projects and outings that put the kids together as a team—not just one on the field or stage, and the rest cheering but separated.

---

[4] Proverbs 17:17 says *a brother is born for adversity*, and a remarkably loyal friend stands out because he is even *closer than a brother* (18:24).

Present but unavailable

When Hal was just out of college, small computers were only able to run a single program at a time. Some smaller apps might be useful several times a day, so to save time, these were loaded into the memory at the startup and left in place after they were finished. The technique was called "Terminate and Stay Resident." And it describes the way many of us interact with our families—we may be physically present, loaded into the family scene if you will, but not really "there." We are present but not available. We're "TSR" to our kids.

We didn't really face how far we'd slipped into this habit ourselves until one of our younger kids, out of the blue, complained, "I hate computers." What boy ever said something like that? But then he explained.

"Everybody sits around with their laptops open, and nobody says anything or does anything anymore."

Ouch. We were guilty as charged, and no excuse.

We love our technology, and it's our main workstation for business, ministry, and volunteer work. For the children, it's frequently their classroom, library, and homework desk. The problem is it's also our platform for entertainment and for fellowship with our friends on social media. We shift from commendable focus on our work and education to idle chat and amusement... completely disregarding the loved ones around us.

We found it helps to have times we all very intentionally unplug. Yes, it's hard; deadlines loom, opportunity knocks, there's a new episode of your favorite video channel to watch. And that just us grownups—when you tell your kids to turn it all off, you have to deal with their whining (which is the audible version of the childish peeve we might be feeling at the same time).

But the more our children become companions and friends, not just housemates and colleagues, the easier the sibling issues become. Investing in time face to face, not just shoulder to shoulder, is worthwhile. Play board games. Go for a walk. Play pickup sports in the yard. Create a family project. Actually visit one of those local museums you've been ignoring. Or even go to a matinee together.

When you take the time to actually be engaged with the ones you're beside, all kinds of discussion happens, memories are built, friendships are forged, and affection grows. It's good for sibling rivalries, and it's good for marriages and families altogether.

How to fight so you both win

When we were engaged, someone introduced us to the idea of a "fair fight." It really is possible to have a disagreement and work to a solution without a trail of broken dishes and scorched landscape. We made a commitment to each other that we'd make a rule of Ephesians 4:26—*Be angry, and yet do not sin; do not let the sun go down on your anger.*[5] We had some late nights the first year or two, but as we worked through our differences and misunderstandings, they came less often. We found that dealing with problems when they were still fresh kept them from becoming large, festering relationship sores.

But this doesn't happen by chance. We had to make a decision to act Biblically and then submit to the Holy Spirit when the conflicts arose. After all, we can just expect that conflicts will occur between two

---

[5] NASB—we were both using the New American Standard Bible when we were engaged and newlyweds.

fallen-but-redeemed sinners. How much more, with the offspring of our union?

Before everyone comes out swinging, we need to ask a critical question—is this worth a disagreement at all? Can I overlook the offense, forgive the offender, and let it pass? The Proverbs tell us, *"The discretion of a man makes him slow to anger, And his glory is to overlook a transgression."*[6] A more homely example is the political consultant's advice to a candidate—"You don't have to kick every dog that barks." Some disagreements are nothing but pettiness or teasing, and if the offended person is willing to ignore it, tolerate, or laugh it off... that may be the better.

But if a disagreement has teeth and needs to be resolved, we shouldn't sweep it aside—we need to deal with it constructively. We've found that a significant part of the parenting we do with our preteens and teens involves coaching them in conflict resolution. There are some fundamental rules we put in place; we never made up a poster or gave them numbers, but we certainly have repeated these standards hundreds of times as our kids stepped on one another's toes, feelings, and boundaries.

Rules of engagement

The goals are to glorify God and restore the relationship. When conflict comes, we don't set out to destroy our opponent and rub his nose in our victory. There may be a legitimate grievance and an actual wrong that needs to be corrected, but our ultimate aim is to honor God and re-establish love and respect by the end. If we both agree with the conclusion, we both win.

No name calling. Names are closely connected to who we are, and we don't allow nicknames that aren't approved by the wearer. (Note,

---

[6] Proverbs 19:11

Mom and Dad can get away with some things that siblings can't, and that's okay!) Jesus warned that hurling an insulting accusation puts the accuser in jeopardy; we don't let our kids call each other "Fool!" but it may be permissible to say, "She's acting foolishly!"[7]

The person is not the problem; their words or actions are. How often has an outraged child come to one of us and sputtered, "You have to do something about *my brother!*" Hal usually tells them, "I can't fix 'your brother.' What did he say or do? That is something we can work on."

Never express your anger physically. In our house dominated by boys, it usually took the form of "Don't hit your brother!" One fundamental fact of our home is you will never be in danger of life or grievous bodily harm from your little sibling; therefore, don't come bleating about "self-defense" when you lashed out at a smaller child.[8] This is crucially important as boys reach their growth spurt. Suddenly they gain significant size and muscle over their close younger sibling, and they genuinely *don't* know their own strength— or the serious consequences of a 150-pound 13-year-old punching a 60-pound sibling.

This restriction against striking out at a person also extends to physical objects. It is strictly *verboten* to slam a door in our house. You don't punch walls, kick the doors, or throw things in frustration, either. Our counsel to our sons has been, when you feel angry, you immediately put your hands *down*.

---

[7] Matthew 5:21-22. It's worth noting that the tone of accusation is important, too, not just the truth of it. See 2 Peter 2:11 and Jude 1:9, as well as Titus 3:2—the word "blasphemy" in Greek means slander and harsh attacks on character, whether of God or of men.

[8] Obviously, the problem of domestic violence is real. We are not talking here about how to respond to true psychotic episodes or physical abuse—these call for professional and police intervention. In most families, sibling rivalry doesn't rise to the level of hospitalization or risk of life.

No extortion or blackmail. "I'm going to tell mom and dad if you don't do what I want you to," doesn't fly at our house. You can't say, "You don't love me!" as part of a fight, either.

Have one fight at a time. The longer a state of conflict goes on, the more issues get pulled into the vortex. This is very typical of marriage stress; we call it the "kitchen sink" effect, where an argument that the mate forgot to mail a bill becomes "You always," and, "You also," "And another thing," and "What's more…" We have to stop listing offenses and deal with them one at a time, to a conclusion, before moving to the next. Paul's description says that love *does not take into account a wrong suffered*; if we follow that rule from Ephesians 4, we avoid building up a laundry list.[9]

Follow Matthew 18. If you're offended with your sister, don't run to Mom or Dad, but go to her privately and give her the chance to make it right. If she doesn't repent, take a witness. If that doesn't work, *then* go to your authority (usually Mom or Dad).[10] This is actually a great help for beleaguered parents. When a child rushes up to call in parental correction ("I need you to lower the boom"), if we ask, "Have you talked about it with your brother yet?" we usually find out the offended child wanted a lightning bolt, not a restoration. He was calling for an air strike, and we sent him back for diplomacy; how unsatisfying. Very often, the problem gets resolved without further intervention from us!

When working it out isn't working

Sometimes, even if they are "trying" to work it out, they just can't seem to do a reasonable job. Kids this age often have a hard time seeing when they are wrong and admitting it

---

[9] 1 Corinthians 13:5 (NASB)—the NIV says *keeps no record of wrongs*. This seems to be a good rendering of the Greek word which other translations assign to "thinking evil" rather than "counting up evils"

[10] Matthew 18:15-17

if they do see it. Remember, their logical processes are not fully developed and their emotions are all over the place. They don't have great judgment. It's not unusual for their idea of an "apology" to be more of an apologetic—an explanation of why they did what they did.[11] Our response is usually, "Um, let's try that again. An apology takes responsibility and asks for forgiveness."

If there is a lot of push back when it comes to taking responsibility for their actions or words, it may be that they don't really believe they're wrong. This is the crux of the situation, because repentance and forgiveness start with admitting you're at fault. If there's resistance, you may need to sit down and talk it out with them, listening to them first, but then taking them to the Word of God and explaining where there is sin or inconsideration or thoughtlessness. At this age, they are a lot more receptive to correction after they've had the opportunity to share their position.

This is *not* an effective way to handle discipline with a younger child. For safety's sake and in obedience to God, a younger child needs to obey first and ask questions later: *Children, obey your parents in the Lord, for this is right... Honor your father and your mother, that it may be well with you and you may live long on the earth.*[12] But a child heading into adolescence needs to be making the transition from parental control to self-control. The way you do that is by talking things out with them. You are not discussing discipline in order to gain their assent or permission—but rather, to give them understanding and a reason to choose the right course later.

---

[11] The English word "apology" has a connotation of repentance, confession, and asking forgiveness. However, the original word, *"apologia"* is a Greek term for a reasoned defense, like a lawyer would give in a courtroom. See Acts 22:1 and 1 Peter 3:15 for examples in the Bible. **Apologetics** then is the branch of theology dealing with evidence and defense of Christianity... and a lawyer defending a client's innocence is presenting an apologetic, not an apology.

[12] Ephesians 6:1, referencing the fifth commandment (Exodus 20:12 and Deuteronomy 5:16)

Stiff-necked and stubborn

W hat about the child who just will not back down, who won't apologize, who won't admit they are wrong? This is so hard! We've been there.

The things that have helped this situation most are listening to them, helping *them* listen to Scripture, and giving them time to listen to the Holy Spirit.

Remember how the enemy seems to tell preteens that no one understands and nobody cares about them? Sometimes this kind of hard-headedness is made worse by a breach in the relationships between the preteen and siblings or parents. One way to heal this is to show them that they're cared for and we're trying to understand. Parents and siblings alike need to hear them out and not rush to judge and correct or lose their tempers with them—hard as it is!

Secondly, bringing them back to the Scriptures can clear a pathway in their heart.

For the word of God is living and powerful, and sharper than any two-edged sword,... and is a discerner of the thoughts and intents of the heart, we're told[13], and God's words have power to reach our kids' souls in a way that our anger and our eloquence don't. God tells us His word *"shall not return to me empty, but it shall accomplish that which I purpose, and shall succeed in the thing for which I sent it."*[14] So we ought to tap into that promise when we need to correct our children.

It's important that we let God's word itself be the sword of the Spirit, and not our hand swinging it. We are all accountable to God, and all of us are His servants and stewards. The Bible's directions and commandments apply to us, too, and we need to *"walk humbly with*

[13] Hebrews 4:12
[14] Isaiah 55:11 (ESV)

our God."[15] When we open the Word to deal with our children's faults, it's a travesty—and ineffectual—for us to berate our kids as if the Bible was *our* weapon against *them.* "You're a murderer, child!" we might say, pointing to the Sermon on the Mount. "See here? Jesus said if you hate someone without cause you've committed murder in your heart. *You're disgusting!*" No.

Did Jesus say that? Yes, indeed. The thoughts and intents of our heart are transparent and visible to God, and He warns us that they have critical moral importance.[16] But the sinless Son of God teaches from a different standing than redeemed-sinner parents. How can we browbeat our children with Scripture without remembering that we are sinners, too, in need of the same daily grace that our children apparently lack?

When there's a major blowup, a multi-car crash on the relationship freeway, we've found it's helpful to sit everyone down, take out our individual Bibles, and take turns reading appropriate verses without a lot of commentary. Calmly help them understand the difficult passages, but let the Word be the main voice heard. It has amazed us how often hearts will soften with very few words from us, when a young person looks up from the printed page and asks, "Hey, can I say something? I was wrong..."[17]

So, when you've heard out their complaints and justifications, and you've gone to the Scriptures for instruction, what if your preteen is still maintaining his innocence? What if she still refuses to bend, repent, or admit any responsibility?

---

[15] Micah 6:8

[16] This is a recurring theme in the Sermon on the Mount, in Matthew 5, 6, and 7—God sees the inner man, and the things we think and do in private have consequences just like outward actions do.

[17] A great resource for this is *For Instruction in Righteousness* by Doorposts. It lists Bible verses for most of the common issues we find in our homes. www.Doorposts.com

We've found it's helpful to give them time to listen to the Holy Spirit, who convicts us of sin. We might ask them to go to their room and think for a while or to go on a walk or to work on something by themselves. They need to be quiet, so don't send them off with a sibling or let them listen to music.

Meanwhile, pray. Pray hard. Examine yourself. Could they really be innocent? We've made some mistakes in our time! Are you making a bigger deal of it than warranted? Is it a disagreement and not a sin? If they are in sin and won't repent, pray even harder because these years are a critical time when they either draw nearer to God or harden their hearts against him.

Your family, the village

Several years ago, a politician who will remain nameless made much of African folk wisdom which said, "It takes a village to raise a child." The phrase became a political football and quickly disappeared in an avalanche of partisan rhetoric.

Politics aside, though, it's clear that God did not intend for human beings to exist in isolation; after all, when He created the first man, He looked at Adam and announced, "*It is not good that man should be alone*," then created the corresponding woman.[18] When He brings children into the arms of the family, He places them in the smallest village—the one which fits around your dinner table. And the raising of each child will involve years of interaction with each member of that tiny community—each of them capable of great mercy and great mischief. The tumultuous years of tweens are just a passing chapter in the longer chronicle; don't despair, make the most of this opportunity to teach and admonish *everyone* in the center of your preteen's life!

---

[18] Genesis 2:18ff

Transitioning 9

One of the difficulties of parenting pre-teens is the problem of simply *classifying* them. It's straightforward enough when you consider young children or teenagers, but where do you put those in-betweeners?

Often, they're promoted from "little kid" to "youth," but that label has its own problems. The common view of "youth" isn't very hopeful; "youth activities" and "youth centers" are proposed as alternatives to gang life and street vagrancy, and even "youth groups" in church are frequently seen as containment areas for young people too immature to sit in the grown-up service.

The Bible doesn't quite seem to match the American view of adolescence. When the apostle Paul wrote to the Corinthian church about maturing in faith, he talked about his own experience growing up.

When I was a child, he said, *I spoke as a child, I understood as a child, I thought as a child; but when I became a man, I put away childish things.*[1]

When you think about our usual views of young people, you might wonder if Paul skipped something. He describes a transition from *childhood* to *adulthood* and doesn't seem to include our culture's vision of the teen years. Where is the time of lazy drifting, the self-centered vagueness, the emotional outbursts, the celebration of foolish and short-sighted behavior? Where's the space for high school romance, youth culture, and all that? Where's the adolescent experience?

---

[1] 1 Corinthians 13:11

No, Paul knew what he meant to say. Frankly, he describes a rather abrupt transition—*when I became a man, I put away childish things.*[2] It suggests that maybe we don't expect enough from our young people—that maybe they're capable of a lot more than we give them credit for.

The Bible *does* talk about youth—it's a real thing. Yet the Bible's view of youth is not like our society's view.

Take, for instance, the case of Timothy. He was Paul's younger co-worker, something of a protégé, and after traveling with the apostle all over the eastern Mediterranean, he planted the church on the island of Crete. Paul, writing as his mentor, advised him:

> *Let no one despise your youth, but be an example to the believers in word, in conduct, in love, in spirit, in faith, in purity.*[3]

Timothy was responsible for founding a church, selecting and training leaders, and serving as the senior pastor of a missionary post in a pagan country. Paul told him to live in such a way that an observer could say, "Aha! That's what a Christian should be like—like young Timothy over there!" Yet he was youthful enough that some wouldn't give him credit for his actual maturity. Paul knew better and encouraged Timothy to be bold where God had placed him.

The Bible's definition of youth includes the very grown-up roles of husband, wife, and parent. Proverbs tells the young man to *"rejoice with the wife of your youth,"*[4] and God warns the wayward husband against dealing falsely with *"the wife of your youth."*[5] Wrapped up in that warning is the blessing of children, and the Psalms underscore

---

[2] 1 Corinthians 13:11
[3] 1 Timothy 4:12. The New American Standard renders it, "*Let no one look down on your youthfulness...*"
[4] Proverbs 5:18
[5] Malachi 2:14-15

that blessing: *"Like arrows in the hand of a warrior, so* are *the children of one's youth."*[6]

And when young David was offended by the taunts of Goliath, King Saul warned him against rushing to accept his challenge:

"You are not able to go against this Philistine to fight him," Saul said, *"for you are a youth, and he a man of war from his youth."*[7]

So the Bible's definition of youth is something larger than ours: "youths" in the Bible are capable of being married, having children—notice the plural in the psalm!—, and serving as soldiers or missionaries. These are things of adulthood, not childhood, and yet these adults are still noted for their youthfulness.

Youth can be capable, but not always

But Saul's caution was not unreasonable. When David confronted the giant on the battlefield, Goliath had the same thought:

And when the Philistine looked about and saw David, he disdained him; for he was only *a youth, ruddy and good-looking.*[8]

Of course, this ended badly for Goliath, but there is a point. People the Bible describes as "youth" may be old enough and mature enough to be married, have children, serve in the military, and even lead churches. On the other hand, "youth" also covers people who still have some growing up to do. There is an element of immaturity or at least, inexperience, in that group.

Take, for example, the sad case of Rehoboam.

Rehoboam became king of Israel at the death of his father, Solomon. The people came to him and asked for relief from the heavy service

---

[6] Psalm 127:4
[7] 1 Samuel 17:33
[8] 1 Samuel 17:42

and taxation Solomon had laid on them. When Rehoboam asked his father's counselors for advice, they told him that a sympathetic response at this point would secure the people's loyalty. But then he turned to *"the young men who had grown up with him and served him,"* and they advised him to show some muscle:

> *"But you shall speak to them, 'My little finger is thicker than my father's loins! Whereas my father loaded you with a heavy yoke, I will add to your yoke; my father disciplined you with whips, but I will discipline you with scorpions.'"*[9]

The Scripture records that when he spoke roughly to the people, they abandoned him—and split the kingdom.

Rehoboam was 41 years old at the time—not exactly a youth by then— but even at that age, he was described as *"young and inexperienced".*[10] It shows that even the elder son of a king, under the parentage of the wisest man who lived, one whose dad and grandfather wrote large parts of the Bible—even that doesn't prevent a young man from growing up immature.

There are other examples in Scripture which suggest that a person may be fully adult and still need the benefit of counsel, mentoring, and instruction. We already looked at Timothy, the youthful church planter who was receiving letters of advice and direction from the apostle Paul. Consider the case of ancient Israel. The first census numbered *"every male individually, from twenty years old and above—all who are able to go to war in Israel."*[11] However, when God assigned the tribe of Levi to serve in the Tabernacle and later the Temple, initially they only served *"from thirty years old and above"*[12]

---

[9] 1 Kings 12:1-16 (NASB)

[10] 2 Chronicles 13:7

[11] Numbers 1:3

[12] Numbers 4:3. It can be noted that the age for service changed through the history of Israel, possibly because the physical demands moderated over time. At the start, the Levites

The same was true of Jesus' earthly ministry. Though at the age of twelve He announced, *"I must be about My Father's business,"*[13] He didn't commence His public mission until He also was thirty years old.[14]

Adult, but still growing

The Biblical pattern, then, suggests that the time we'd call "youth" can be fully adult in terms of responsibility and expectations, and yet still growing in wisdom and experience.

Where does that lead us today, here?

Once place it does *not* lead us is to conclude marriage at 14 is A-OK, as an example. Our time and place doesn't adapt well to independent adulthood until someone reaches 18—or 21, in some things. Marriage is one area; work and career are another; and you can think of other things that a young teen really couldn't manage in our society.

But it does encourage us to consider that young teenagers may be able to do a lot more than we thought. Our own grandparents talked about doing meaningful work alongside their parents, often the same tasks the "grown-ups" were doing, as ten—or twelve-year-olds. We often share the story of Admiral David Farragut, the Civil War naval hero; he began his service as a midshipman at the age of nine, and in the War of 1812 was given command of a captured British whaler—at eleven years old. John Quincy Adams, the sixth president, began his public service as the official translator for the American mission to the court of the Russian empress Catherine the Great, at the age of fourteen. The beloved Laura Ingalls Wilder was a certified

---

were responsible for some heavy physical labor assembling, packing, and transporting the structures and furniture of the tabernacle.

[13] Luke 2:49
[14] Luke 3:23

teacher instructing a classroom, when she was barely sixteen—and still a high school student herself.

With capability comes responsibility. The historical examples above convince us that teenagers, sometimes young teenagers, and maybe even pre-teens, are capable of taking on serious roles if they're properly trained, properly supported, and properly supervised. Sure, at their age, the mature adults in the area will want to check on things and make sure they're happening, but the point is that very young adults need to start *somewhere*—and now is the time to begin.

Establishing a new vision

This idea will probably come as a surprise to many parents. The common view of kids this age, not to mention the teenagers they're about to become, sets a very, very low bar. Adopting this counter-cultural view of our own pre-teens and teens will put us on a less-traveled road.

Yet we believe this is a key to understanding our young people as they move from undisputed childhood toward the fully-capable, independent adulthood we hope for. It's encouraging to us as parents, and it's encouraging to them as fledgling adults, to say, "This boy, this girl, these young people are on their way. They are going places, not wasting time. God has created them for a positive purpose in His kingdom. And we can help prepare them without interfering in their growth or holding them back."

We'll share some ideas how parents can help establish this vision in subsequent chapters—how to instill it in your kids, how to explain it to your family, and how to work it out in the community around you. But for now, we want to encourage you as the parents to have greater expectations—tempered with grace, mercy, and reality—of your pre-teens, wherever they are in their pathway of transition!

Celebrating Growth 10

L ife is hard, but sometimes we don't know any better. When our young family was growing, we frequently heard from older people who warned how poor they'd been growing up in a large Depression-era family—but then wistfully added, "But my brothers and sisters and I had so much fun together!"

Melanie's grandfather and his twin brother were the youngest of a family of eleven kids. When they finished eighth grade, his father looked at the two of them and said the family couldn't afford for both to go to high school; one would need to start working to help support the rest. He made them flip a coin to decide. Telling the story decades later, Melanie's grandfather would say, with delight in his eyes, "And I won!"—meaning he joined his many relatives who walked to the cotton mill every morning. Even after years of struggle, he looked back with a fourteen-year-old's thrill at stepping into the shoes of manhood at last.

In cultures all around the world and for much of human history, the transition from childhood to a new young adult status has had a formal recognition. There is clearly a breakpoint in the early teens where a new man or new woman is emerging, and society takes notice. It's only appropriate that the community mark this event in a memorable way.

There is a two-fold problem in American culture, though. On the one hand, we have an obsession with youthfulness that led to a toleration of behavior that used to be called childish but now meets with a shrug as "sad, but normal." At the same time, the lengthening of the years of formal schooling, joined with restrictions against younger teens doing any meaningful work or taking other steps toward adult responsibility, have erased some of the natural thresholds. Growing up that used to happen at 12 or 13 is pushed off to 18 or even 21.

One community preserved it

One exception to this change is the traditional Jewish celebration of the *bar mitzvah*. At the age of thirteen, a Jewish boy is officially welcomed into the synagogue and community. The term means, "Son of the Law," to underscore that from this point on, the young man takes responsibility for his own obedience to God. As a *bar mitzvah*, he now counts as part of the synagogue quorum or *minyan* and he's invited to take part in synagogue affairs. He's one of the men now—though admittedly, still young and inexperienced. A Jewish girl, likewise, can look forward to becoming a *bat mitzvah*—when she becomes a "Daughter of the Law" at twelve.

We think there's some value to this. Psychologists Joseph and Claudia Allen, in their book *Escaping the Endless Adolescence*, relate that many in their field are saying that the time of adolescence now continues into the early thirties, and "Twenty-five is the new fifteen." Sadly, the level of maturity we used to see in teenagers is all that is expected of twenty-somethings today. That's not what we want for our children.

Instead of accepting this declining cultural norm, we thought it made better sense to call our sons and daughters to step up for more adult responsibility rather than settle back for an extended childhood

So when our children turn 12 or 13, we hold a formal welcome to young adulthood, and throw a celebration alongside. Just like the *bar mitzvah* tradition, it's a time both serious and joyful. However, as Christians we are not under law but under grace, and since we hope that our sons and daughters are growing in the knowledge and experience of God's grace, we call our celebration a *"Bar Chanon"* or *"Bat Chanon"* ceremony—as they become a son or daughter of grace.

In keeping with that recognition of grace, not law, we have to interject here that there is no commandment to have such an observance. The Bible mentions at times that there are milestones in life and suggests that at some point, young men and women should be respected as adults and expected to take on adult responsibility, but there is not a specific ritual or celebration mentioned at this point. The Jewish ceremony dates from the Middle Ages, based on older Talmudic traditions.

But though it's not a commandment, we do think it's valuable to formally recognize that transition and encourage us all to be aiming for it. As parents, we need to be preparing our children to be adults, giving them increasing responsibility and the independence that comes with it. Our kids need to see themselves as adults in training and begin to take responsibility for themselves, their belongings, and their future. Older siblings need to learn not to treat the new teen as a child, but to welcome them into a new phase of life. Younger siblings need to understand that their older brother or sister may have more to answer for than they do. Having a formal ceremony reminds us all of those things.

But whether or not you observe this transition in a formal way, or how you observe it, you're at liberty. If you decide to do something to mark the occasion, you can include all kinds of things in your celebration. Here's how we approach it.

What kind of ceremony?

Some of the earliest questions to answer are what kind of ceremony do you want to have ... and what does that tell you about the invitation list?

Many cultures have initiation rituals designed for the men of the family and tribe. The elders take the young man (or groups of them) away from the home community and conduct their ceremonies in a male-only environment. After all, the focus is on the transition from boyhood to manhood; what is more natural than surrounding the young candidate with the men who represent the world he's about to enter? Other cultures have similar traditions for the young women and their female relatives; older women in the clan help the young lady fulfill traditions which are supposed to make her a fruitful, wise, energetic woman and good mother.

Some families we know do a men-only or women-only ceremony with a Christian perspective; others make it even more intimate. Two of our friends make one-on-one trips with their sons, for instance. One dad, a corporate executive, takes his sons to an upscale, out-of-town hotel like he frequently visits and the only business for this trip is father-and-son. Another takes his sons on a wilderness retreat, camping and hiking between times of prayer and conversation—like Jesus and His disciples.

We've taken a different approach—we make it a family occasion. We'll get significant men to counsel and challenge our sons, and women of importance to speak to our daughters, but we include all ages and generations in the celebration. It's important to us to make a public statement of the new responsibilities being assumed by this young adult, and make a public announcement of the change in status we are now conferring. Though he or she will always be one of our "boys" or "girls," we won't be counting them among the "little ones" and "kids." We want others to hold him (and us) to account, and encourage him to embrace his new role.

What advice would you give a young adult?

One of the things we want our young men and women to take away from the ceremony is that higher expectations aren't just their parents' notion—it's part of growing into maturity. It's powerful for them to hear wisdom from many people, not just Mom and Dad, and especially when you hear the same truths your parents have taught echoed in the words of people across the community.

The way you present those voices can take whatever form you like. What suits your sense of style or propriety?

Some families adopt symbolic rituals like nobles used to confer knighthood on a squire—even administering the traditional accolade with a long sword, which is then presented to the young man. (Historically, knighthood was sometimes conferred by the king, who approached the candidate and soundly boxed his ears. We don't recommend this practice!)

Others assign their young people to long periods of preparation and study, challenging them to memorize passages of Scripture or catechisms, or to prepare a speech or message to deliver at the ceremony.

We use a less elaborate form, focusing on words of welcome, exhortation, and encouragement to the young man or lady. In our ceremonies, we invite several men or women of significance in the young person's life to prepare short presentations about what it means to be a man or woman. These will each focus on a character trait and some point of wisdom which the speaker has learned. We encourage the adults we invite to ask themselves, "What do you wish you had known when you were 13?"

We also encourage them to bring an inexpensive gift as an object lesson to illustrate their point. This can be a lot of fun for all concerned. Some examples we've seen:

A small pair of binoculars like a hunter would use to spot and identify his quarry. The lesson was that a man should be visionary, looking to the road ahead, and seeking counselors to help him understand things he hasn't seen himself.

A string of decorative lights, as a reminder to keep the light of Christ bright in her life

An antique carpenter's plane, from a relative's collection of handmade tools. The lesson was how a man's gifts and skills can be used constructively, to build and to beautify useful objects, but the same skills can be abused and turned into destructive ends.

A nice journal for Bible study and prayer notes—with obvious applications!

A folding multi-tool. A man should be prepared for all kinds of situations!

In our family, the culminating presentation is always given by their parents. Since we expect the young adult to take more responsibility for his or her own spiritual walk, we encourage them to be active students of the Word, and on this occasion present them with a leather-bound study Bible like we parents use. This actually is a follow up to an earlier gift—when each of our children learns to read, we celebrate the achievement with a large-print presentation Bible of their own. The inexpensive Bible we give them at age 6 or 7 recognizes that young children can be pretty careless with their belongings; by the time they're 12 or 13, the old Bible is pretty worn, and a high-quality replacement has double meaning to them!

Who does the speaking?

We think it's only natural for the young man to be welcomed into the adult community by the voices of the older men he will be joining. When it's time for our daughters to step into the ranks of young women, we have a similar focus on older women teaching the younger.

But who should you consider including?

The ones we invite to speak are adults who have some connection and significance in the young adult's life already. Obviously, for our young men, we included Hal, the father, as the closest man and role model in their life. From there, you can include grandfathers, uncles, men and leaders in the church, and others like parents of friends, coaches, or teachers outside the immediate family. For our daughters, we include their mother Melanie, plus grandmothers, aunts, women of the church, parents of friends, and others they have a relationship with.

What about family members who don't share your convictions? It may be hard on family relationships if certain people were excluded, but what if inviting them might make a mockery of the occasion?

We learned a surprising lesson at our wedding. We were both believers and planned a very Christ-centered ceremony. One of our extended family was married to a militant atheist, and nobody was quite sure what to expect from him at our very Christian event. To our surprise, he volunteered for a key role in the weekend's events, and we caught him on the video, singing the hymns with gusto. We've realized on many occasions that there is often a desire to be part of something above the mundane part of life, and even non-religious people may respond to the tone and intention of a serious event.

One way to help them feel comfortable in the unfamiliar situation is to schedule their presentation late in the ceremony. They'll be able to observe the tone of the earlier speakers' remarks, and adjust their own to be in keeping with the flow of the ceremony. They'll also have a feel for how long to speak, and how to pace their remarks. No one likes to feel awkward, and generally, we think, people will grasp the seriousness you place on the occasion and will try to act accordingly.

It helps to remember that the experience of growing up and assuming the roles of manhood and womanhood is not exclusive to any faith, culture, or philosophy. Someone whose personal code is quite at odds with your own may still share useful experience about the value of integrity, diligence, work-life balance, health, or financial management. Even someone with a broken relationship in his past may have some hard-won lessons to share. If you have reason for concern, you might phrase your invitation as a request to share on a particular subject: "Uncle Bob, I've always admired the hard work you put in to pay your way through college. Would you be willing to share a few thoughts on the benefits of going the extra length to stay out of debt?"

What if a generation is missing? Both our fathers passed away before we were married, so there were no grandfathers to invite for our sons' ceremonies. Instead, we asked our mothers to speak as representatives of the family's older generation. We have been blessed with their contribution to the ceremony!

One surprise blessing came when we included older brothers in the mix. Young people are growing and changing so rapidly during the teen years, even a two—or three-year gap between the guest of honor and his big brother or older sister can yield real insights. Our sons are all close in age and affection, and the older ones have been delighted to share even their few years' perspective with their younger brother. As parents, you can help an uneasy speaker with his preparation, but do include them. The things their brothers have said are among our favorite memories.

Don't overlook the celebration!

n the serious business of initiating your child into the mysterious world of adulthood, it's easy to let the celebration slip from view. Is that even important?

Actually, we'd say it's quite Biblical. Even occasions of great solemnity in Scripture came with times of feasting, rich food, and sweet beverages. We want our children to reach out for their new roles with a sense of excitement and joy—and we want to invite our friends and family to "rejoice with those who rejoice"!

As a family with eight children, we were sensitive to the large footprint we could leave on a small community's social calendar, so we decided to make birthday parties small, family-centered affairs— just the ten of us at home, plus whatever grandparents were nearby. This party, though, is the biggest of the birthdays—we talk about it and plan it for months or years before the Big Date occurs. Unlike the other birthdays, this one really is meant to be a public occasion.

We found it works well to have the entertainment portion before the food. What form that entertainment takes, though, is just as varied as your son's or daughter's imagination. We let the young people do most of the planning (with advice and consent of the parents) for location, activities, and food, and It has been interesting to see how the event reflects the young person:

One son hosted a hymn sing.

Another asked for a simple time of unstructured fellowship with friends and their families.

Our daughter hosted a formal tea for all her friends and their families.

Another son who enjoyed the games of Ultimate Frisbee™ he played with the young adults after church, asked to organize the biggest game of Ultimate he could imagine (over sixty players took part, in the area of three soccer fields!)

Yet another worked with friends in the country to hold a turkey shoot on their rural property. (If you're not familiar with this custom, it's a traditional target shooting competition still common in the South. The Cary Grant movie *Sergeant York* illustrated the old-fashioned form using a live turkey; we followed the modern custom using paper targets and awarded a Walmart gift card.)

For locations, we've used the church fellowship hall, a friend's back yard, our own home, or a city park.

For food, you could do anything from simple punch and cake, to a catered sit-down dinner. We've had buffet style (even pot luck) dinners, but a cook-out format works well with our full-family invitation; the expense is manageable, it's easy to ask guests to bring side dishes, desserts, or beverages, and the usual outdoor venue makes cleanup easy and spills no problem. Our daughter, though, wanted something a bit more formal. She asked that we do a high tea. It was an amazing experience to do together.

By planning the entertainment first, the meal or refreshment preparation can take place in the background while the younger guests, especially, have more interesting things to do (and therefore, there's less crowding while the helpers are setting up the food). As the food wraps up, we move to the ceremonial part with the presentations, and then close with prayer. The early busyness followed by food helps the little ones work off some energy and then settle down in time for the quieter part of the program.

Invitations

Invitations to your coming of age celebration can be simple or formal. They can be emailed, hand delivered, posted online or sent through the Post Office. They all need to include the same things: the occasion, the host, the honoree (that's your new young adult), and the date, time, and place.

We like using formal language to help people understand that this is an event that is important to us. Any traditional guide to etiquette would have templates for this; look at advice for a formal wedding if you're unsure! This is the sort of language we've used:

Mr. & Mrs. John Q. Public

Request the Pleasure of Your Company

And That of Your Family

At the Bar Chanon Celebration

of

Their Son

Jason Quincy Public

On June 2, 2018

At 3pm

At Centennial Park

Smalltown, Georgia

The Favor of a Reply is Requested.

Formal invitations often include the acronym RSVP for "*Répondez, s'il vous plaîs*," — "Reply, please" in French. We prefer to write that out in English since so few people seem to understand that RSVP requires a response anymore![1]

We like to try to make the invitations personalized for each of our children. For example, one of our sons' invitations recalled a fun memory from when we had all boys. Whenever it was time to leave, we'd call them with the old cavalry command, "Boots and saddles!" — meaning "Get your shoes and get in the van!" We used an engraving of cavalry troopers mounting their steeds to reflect that family tradition.

Another son loved birds of prey—falcons, eagles, raptors of all sorts. We wanted an invitation that he would love, so we created one in a more contemporary style with a photo of a golden eagle as a background. His younger brother loved the age of chivalry, so for the background of his invitation, we used a painting of a knight receiving his accolade.

---

[1] To be quite honest, it is common now for people to ignore this request, which can make planning quite difficult. Having successfully completed seven "*Chanon*" celebrations and catered the groom's side of a recent wedding ourselves, our best advice is to maximize your own flexibility for the event. A buffet or cookout in an expansive location will help you absorb a few extra guests. If you have significant absences, you may have leftover food to share with others or take home for yourselves; you might want to consider that possibility in your planning as well.

There are plenty of websites which offer free stock photographs and public-domain artwork, and you can drop images into a word processor or add text to a picture with a graphic program—whatever your skill set and creativity allow! Or you might choose to be completely up to date and use an online invitation program or just a simple email to your whole church.

Whatever method you use, just be sure to send invitations out a few weeks in advance—or longer, if your date is near a holiday or vacation season.

Explanations

Although the idea of an intentional coming-of-age ceremony seems to be gaining in popularity, at this point it is still likely many of your guests won't understand quite what they have been invited to! Your choice of invitation style and wording will give a clue to the larger group of guests, but for the speaking participants, we've found it helpful to attach a brief explanation of the reason for the event and their prospective role in it. This is a typical message we've used for our sons' events:

Dear Friends,

Our son, _____ (has just celebrated / will soon celebrate) his thirteenth birthday. We believe it is important to establish milestones in the life of a young man, and this year is a time traditionally recognized as the threshold of adult life. We are planning to set aside a time of celebration and reflection to mark this as a special day in his life. We would like to invite your family to join with ours on this occasion, to share a meal, fellowship, and a time of challenge and encouragement for _____.

The Jewish *bar mitzvah* ceremony calls a boy to begin the transformation from childhood to maturity, becoming a "son of the Law". Since we are not under the law of Moses but the grace of Christ, our family desires each of our boys to become a "son of grace"—a *bar chanon*—with the similar expectation that he begin to put away childish things, prepare himself for the responsibilities of manhood, and pursue his own relationship with God. Doing an event like this certainly isn't in any way required, but we believe it will have a large impact on our son and become a cherished memory for him.

As a part of this celebration, we would appreciate it if the men of each family (and his older brothers and grandmothers) would prepare a short exhortation for _____, and if you wish, a small gift as an object lesson and memorial to him. Consider what you wish someone would have told you as you embarked on young manhood. One example might be the responsibility of a man to use his strength and diligence to work, build, and provide for himself and his family, but also warning that his strength can be misused to injure and destroy. It is only in conscious submission to the will of God that a man will be productive in His kingdom. An object lesson might involve a hammer or some other tool.

We don't want this to be a burden to anyone—two to five minutes of sharing, and nothing expensive or elaborate necessary— because the focus is on your wisdom and counsel. Each of you has been a friend to our family and to _____, and we appreciate your advice for our son.

For our friends and family who are too far away to join us, we would love to have something from you to read aloud to _____ at the party. Please email us anything you'd like to share with him.

For those that can attend, we'll be (grilling hamburgers and hot dogs). If you'd like to bring a side dish and a drink, that would be great! Dress is casual. Please take a look at the attached invitation for details and let us know as soon as possible if you will be able to attend so that we can plan the food. You can easily reply to our invitation here: <Link to Google Form>

In Christ,

(signed)

Keeping track of guests

We used an online form that allows guests to respond with how many people they are bringing, what ages they'll be, and what food items they are bringing, too. That allows us to plan how much food to buy and what paper products we'll need. We've put together an editable form you are welcome to save a copy for your own use or, of course, you can design your own.[2]

Make sure your invitation goes out early enough that people can save the date and you have a good turnout. We often fail to plan things soon enough and it makes them harder to pull off. We suggest getting invitations out at least a month in advance.

Walking it out

We've talked about why a formal "coming of age" ceremony can be useful in a modern Christian family. We discussed ideas about who to invite, who to have as a presenter, and

---

[2] http://goo.gl/forms/6p8JWCjgJP Be sure to click the three dots in the upper right hand corner and Save a Copy so that you are not inputting your information into the form everyone can see!

what sort of presentation to have. Last, we talked about the role of celebration—what sort of entertainment and fellowship you might include. After all, the event is not all solemnity and teaching—it's rejoicing at our child's next step toward maturity!

At the end of the day, though, the whole point of the ceremony is not just a special event for a day or a weekend—it's a milestone along a pathway to independent adulthood. And guess what—this is where the parents really get to shine.

The reason we have this celebration, after all, is to make a statement to the public and to our own family that our son or daughter has entered a new stage of life. That means things will be different for him or her from now on. Now it's the parent's responsibility to start making that a reality.

We know that maturity doesn't happen with the 18th birthday, or the 21st, or especially the 13th. It's a process of training, growth, and correction we call "growing up"! And it takes time and effort.

As we've walked down this road with our own children, we've find this gateway event helps us focus on the change in our parenting relationship, and it helps our children embrace the transition they will be making as they step into full independence just a few short years later. Maybe a formal recognition of this sort will do the same things in your family!

Producers, Not Consumers

11

enjamin Franklin, one of our founding fathers, is remembered for his homespun advice and folksy wisdom. Through *Poor Richard's Almanack*, he permanently added to American culture old English proverbs like "Early to bed and early to rise, Makes a man healthy, wealthy and wise." He was well known for his frugality and regular habits, as well as his wit and curiosity.

His interest in thrift got a very early start. In a letter to a friend, Ben Franklin tells a story he was fond of recounting:

> In my Opinion we might all draw more Good, from it than we do, & suffer less Evil, if we would but take care not to give too much for our Whistles. For to me it seems that most of the unhappy People we meet with, are become so by Neglect of that Caution.

> You ask what I mean? —You love Stories, and will excuse my telling you one of my self.

> When I was a Child of seven Years old, my Friends on a Holiday fill'd my little Pocket with Halfpence. I went directly to a Shop where they sold Toys for Children; and being charm'd with the Sound of a Whistle that I met by the way, in the hands of another Boy, I voluntarily offer'd and gave all my Money for it. When I came home, whistling all over the House, much pleas'd with my Whistle, but disturbing all the Family, my Brothers, Sisters & Cousins, understanding the Bargain I had made, told me I had given four times as much for it as

it was worth, put me in mind what good Things I might have bought with the rest of the Money, & laught at me so much for my Folly that I cry'd with Vexation; and the Reflection gave me more Chagrin than the Whistle gave me Pleasure.

This however was afterwards of use to me, the Impression continuing on my Mind; so that often when I was tempted to buy some unnecessary thing, I said to myself, Do not give too much for the Whistle; and I sav'd my Money.

As I grew up, came into the World, and observed the Actions of Men, I thought I met many who gave too much for the Whistle.

When I saw one ambitious of Court Favour, sacrificing his Time in Attendance at Levees, his Repose, his Liberty, his Virtue and perhaps his Friend, to obtain it; I have said to myself, This Man gives too much for his Whistle.

When I saw another fond of Popularity, constantly employing himself in political Bustles, neglecting his own Affairs, and ruining them by that Neglect, He pays, says I, too much for his Whistle.

If I knew a Miser, who gave up every kind of comfortable Living, all the Pleasure of doing Good to others, all the Esteem of his Fellow Citizens, & the Joys of benevolent Friendship, for the sake of Accumulating Wealth, Poor Man, says I, you pay too much for your Whistle.

When I met with a Man of Pleasure, sacrificing every laudable Improvement of his Mind or of his Fortune, to mere corporeal Satisfactions, & ruining his Health in their Pursuit, Mistaken Man, says I, you are providing Pain for your self instead of Pleasure, you pay too much for your Whistle.

If I see one fond of Appearance, of fine Cloaths, fine Houses, fine Furniture, fine Equipages, all above his Fortune, for which he contracts

Debts, and ends his Career in a Prison; Alas, says I, he has paid too much for his Whistle.

When I saw a beautiful sweet-temper'd Girl, marry'd to an ill-natured Brute of a Husband; What a Pity, says I, that she should pay so much for a Whistle!

In short, I conceiv'd that great Part of the Miseries of Mankind, were brought upon them by the false Estimates they had made of the Value of Things, and by their giving too much for the Whistle.

Yet I ought to have Charity for these unhappy People, when I consider that with all this Wisdom of which I am boasting, there are certain things in the World so tempting; for Example the Apples of King John, which happily are not to be bought, for if they were put to sale by Auction, I might very easily be led to ruin my self in the Purchase, and find that I had once more given too much for the Whistle.

Adieu, my dearest Friend, and believe me ever yours very sincerely and with unalterable Affection.

Benjamin Franklin

November 29, 1779[1]

At the age of 73, Franklin could still look back at his childish impulsiveness and feel annoyed with himself. Just as his adult character was shaped by this moment of foolishness, our preteens are shaping their adult views of finance right now. Did you know tweens, as the marketers call them, are considered a plum market? If you search on marketing to tweens, or preteens as consumers, or anything like that, article after article comes up explaining that

---

[1] "From Benjamin Franklin to Madame Brillon: Letter and Printed Bagatelle ("The Whistle"), 10 November 1779," *Founders Online,*National Archives, last modified July 12, 2016, http://founders.archives.gov/documents/Franklin/01-31-02-0041. [Original source: *The Papers of Benjamin Franklin,* vol. 31, *November 1, 1779, through February 29, 1780,* ed. Barbara B. Oberg. New Haven and London: Yale University Press, 1995, pp. 69-77.]

preteens wield more economic power than ever before and that they
are forming brand loyalties that will follow them into adulthood.
Businesses are admonished to consider them in their advertising
and even their store design.

The thing is, we don't want our kids to see themselves as consumers.
We want them to understand money from a Biblical perspective.
Like Franklin, we don't want our progeny to pay too much for their
whistles, especially when they become adults.

It's not that money is evil. People say, "Money is the root of all evil,"
but the actual verse says, *For the love of money is a root of all kinds of
evils. It is through this craving that some have wandered away from the
faith and pierced themselves with many pangs.*[2] The problem is not money
itself but loving it so much you are turned away from serving God.
Money should not be an idol in our lives, and it can sneak up on us
if we aren't careful.

It's not ours to begin with

We have to remember to teach our children that everything
belongs to God. *Indeed heaven and the highest heavens belong
to the Lord your God, also the earth with all that is in it.*[3] All
the wealth we call our own is included in that. *For every beast of the
forest is Mine, And the cattle on a thousand hills.*[4]

If all the wealth in the world is God's, then the wealth we control is
not by ownership but by stewardship. A steward is responsible for
managing his master's affairs; when Joseph was a slave in Egypt, his
service was so reliable that his master *left all that he had in Joseph's
charge, and because of him he had no concern about anything but the food*

---

[2] 1 Timothy 6:10 ESV, emphasis added.
[3] Deuteronomy 10:14
[4] Psalm 50:10

he ate.[5] A faithful steward might have great liberty with the things in his care—Joseph himself remarked that he had free reign with everything but the master's wife![6]—but he always knows that he's accountable to the true owner.

Whether we are rich or poor, we're responsible to God for managing His belongings with care. It's important that whether we're thinking of finances, time, personal talents, or spiritual gifts, we train our children to invest them well for the glory of God.[7]

Understanding money and work

We recently read through the *Little House* series with our younger children. Though most of the story follows the childhood of Laura Ingalls Wilder, the book *Farmer Boy* describes the early life of Almanzo Wilder, whom she eventually married.

In one chapter, nine-year-old Almanzo is at the Independence Day fair with his cousins and friends. The town boys tease him because he doesn't have the money to buy lemonade, and when he blusters that he only needs to ask his father for it, he ends up taking a dare to do just that. Almanzo's father sees what's going on, and instead of giving him a few pennies for a treat, gave the boy a whole half dollar—a huge amount for a child in 1855! Before he goes, though, Father reminds him that a half dollar is about what they got for a bushel of potatoes. He walks Almanzo through the whole process again of preparing the fields, planting the seed potatoes, cultivating, harvesting, and sorting the best for sale. That half dollar represented the work that went into producing one bushel of potatoes.

---

[5] Genesis 39:6 ESV
[6] Genesis 39:9
[7] The classic example is Jesus' parable of the talents, Matthew 25:14-30.

That's a basic lesson of economics. We write books for a living, but the power company won't let us pay our electrical bill in boxes of books. Sometimes we trade a few books with another author, but we can't leave an armload of books to pay for a tank of gas. If we grew potatoes or turnips or grass-fed beef, we can't pay our property taxes with a truck load of farm products. And if we were attorneys, we couldn't pay our doctor bills with free legal consultation... if the doctor had no need of our service! Instead, we convert our books or beef or legal briefs into money and that money stands for the work we've done and the things we produced.

After Papa Wilder teaches Almanzo about the value of money, he tells him that he is welcome to the half dollar in recognition of all the work he did. He can spend it as he liked. However, almost as an afterthought, he suggested that a half dollar could buy a suckling pig. If Almanzo raised that pig until it had a litter of its own, he could raise those pigs and sell them for four or five dollars each. Or, he could go drink as many glasses of lemonade as he could possibly want... and the money would be all gone. Almanzo invested in a piglet that day!

That's a valuable lesson to our kids in the difference between being a consumer and being a producer. Almanzo could take the value of all that work and "drink it all up," as his dad said, or he could invest it to produce something of more value. He could also save it, letting it grow by interest or until he'd put aside enough for a larger purchase, or he could give it away to someone in need or to support the Lord's work. There are many ways to be a good steward. Sometimes, spending is appropriate as we enjoy the good gifts God has given us. Sometimes investing or saving or giving is the best thing to do.

Where's it coming from?

H ow do preteens get the money businesses are working so hard to entice them to spend?

Most of them get money from allowances, gifts, or being paid to work. Which is the best way? It depends on your circumstances.

When Hal was a boy, his family gave him an allowance. It was small enough that he would have to save for several weeks if he wanted something significant. Later, in high school, Hal worked as a dishwasher in a local pizzeria.

Melanie's family was in business for themselves and she worked right alongside them. If she needed money for anything, her parents just gave it to her since she had helped to earn it. She didn't work outside the family until she was in college.

We've done a variety of things with our children over the years. We gave allowances for a few years, until a change of circumstances made it impractical. Naturally they receive gifts from relatives at Christmas and birthdays, and they've done odd jobs and later, run their own businesses. By and large, we've found it was best when they've earned what they spend.

Some families pay their children for certain work, either in the home or in the family business. Our rule has been that tasks we might hire out—yard work, for instance—we might be willing to pay our kids for. But there are some tasks around the house and property that we consider part of living together as a family. No one pays the parents to cook, do laundry, or take out the trash. All of us pitch in to keep the household running, and everyone learns as many household tasks as they can. If we parents put a cash reward on every little chore, we can create the mindset that a job isn't worth a child's attention until the money's right. That's not the spirit of service we want to encourage in our home.

Shopping as education

Remember that Jesus taught His disciples by example explained. He went out to teach and minister to the people, then He returned to His twelve and asked, "Did you see what I did? Do you understand what I was saying?" He didn't expect them to learn by deduction; He took them along as he went about His mission, but He came back to explain the significance of His words and actions.

The training of our young disciples works the same way. If we want to teach them about stewardship, how to manage God's money in our care, then we explain it as we live it out.

Naturally the younger kids tag along on errands, just as a matter of managing your family life... but have you ever talked with them about how you're shopping, not just the fact, "We're going to the grocery store to get milk"?

Even when they're small, you can begin to explain how you make selections. Do they understand the difference between value and price? In our household, we don't make distinction between brands of milk, eggs, or saltines; as far as we can tell, these are commodities and there is little difference between the brands. Price is our guide, and we get whatever's cheapest! But when it comes to ketchup, for a long time we had an understanding that we would pay the difference in price to get one of the major brands. Store brands have improved since we were married, but for many years, there was enough of a difference in flavor and enjoyment that we would buy the more expensive ketchup, and make up the savings on other items. We valued better ketchup more than we valued the extra few cents of higher price.

Your own tastes will guide the discussion with *your* kids!

As they gain more understanding of math, you can explain how quantity makes a difference, when a five-pound "family package" of hamburger is cheaper per pound than a two-pound tray. You can even point out how stores use loss leaders to bring customers into their stores, hoping the customer who chooses their shop for the special deal on chicken will buy the rest of the family list there at the regular price.

Preteens should already be able to handle purchases with their own cash. By the time they reach this stage, you should be teaching them how to make purchases with a debit card (explaining the importance of keeping the PIN secret) and giving them opportunities to make purchases without your supervision.

Even if your family doesn't use credit cards, you need to talk to your preteens about credit. Most of us will take out a mortgage, finance a car, or take out a student loan for college, so our kids need to understand how financing works. Sooner or later your young person is likely to have a credit card issued by an employer for travel or business supplies. Credit card companies reach out to kids beginning in their teens and stalk college campuses, so your preteen needs to learn what is really being offered and the potential down side of the business.

Our short answer is that credit is like fire—a useful servant but a terrible master. Interest is just the rent you pay on the money you borrow, and if you pay your balance in full each month, you will never see an interest charge. Any balance that remains, though, will cost you.

We get our young people a credit card on our account when they begin driving. We give them the instructions, "This is to allow you to buy gas for the car, or to pay when we send you to the store." And we set the stage for instruction by giving them permission to use the card for personal items, with the understanding the payment is due when the monthly bill is posted.

(cue ominous music)

This arrangement usually works for a month or two, until the Day of Reckoning comes and the teen realizes he's been to the coffee house a couple of times more than he thought, and Income did not match Expenses on his account. At that point, we politely require as much repayment as they're able, and explain that since the Proverbs tell us *the borrower is servant to the lender*,[8] they should consider themselves, and any income, as servants to their parental creditors.

One of our teens ran up a $146 bill that way, and the experience of working it off gave him such a horror of debt, he worked multiple jobs and lived in a seedy student apartment while in college—and graduated on time and debt free. We consider that a success story!

Be sure to explain how checking accounts work, too. The Federal Reserve System reports that checks have largely been replaced by debit and credit cards, and less than 5% of all transactions now involve a physical check.[9] Still, there are times and places where a check is expected or appropriate, and your kids need to know how to write them and more importantly, how they're handled by the bank.

Several years ago, a young woman we know planned to go Christmas shopping for her friends at college. She called her bank to check her balance, and then happily wrote small checks all over town. Unfortunately, she didn't realize the bank only knew about checks

---

[8] Proverbs 22:7
[9] *The Federal Reserve Payments Study 2016*, The Federal Reserve System, December 2016. https://www.federalreserve.gov/newsevents/press/other/2016-payments-study-20161222.pdf Accessed March 4, 2018.

received *at the bank*, not the big one that was still outstanding... and she bounced several checks. The fees and penalties were more than the Christmas shopping.

Checks remain the one form of payment that doesn't process immediately, and we need to make sure our kids remember that little quirk!

The family budget

When Hal was young, his family didn't really talk much about the family finances. He remembers seeing survey cards in magazines, asking about household income, and feeling scandalized—that was *private!* Melanie's family took a much more open approach and she remembers balancing the family and business checking accounts as a young teen.

There's no real right or wrong here, but there are some advantages to letting your kids in on the family finances. You don't have to give them all the details, but even a nine-year-old can understand that money isn't limitless and spending has priorities. When we say, "We can't afford that," and they know that we don't indulge ourselves with impulse purchases, we're modeling good financial behavior.

What if your past decisions have created problems for your family? Maybe you're struggling to finish off student loans, or you ran up your credit cards and found they take a *long* time to pay off at the minimums, or you took on too big a mortgage before the market downturn? Don't be afraid to talk about it. We need to remember that God appointed us to be parents, not because we were smart or good looking or holier than the next couple, but simply in His gracious will. He knew our failures and sins before we were born, so the fact we made bad financial moves in the past doesn't cancel our responsibility to teach our kids a better way. Our children know us better than we realize, and we've found that being honest about our mistakes and sharing even our unpleasant experiences actually receives a surprising amount of grace from our kids. It gives credibility to our warnings!

Countercultural

The marketers really want to encourage our families to buy more and bigger—especially our impressionable kids. Of course, that's the marketers' job; on the other hand, we want our kids to see themselves more as *producers* than *consumers*. Consumers are focused on buying, on getting more and more stuff. A consumer acquires value or consumes it. In contrast, producers contribute to the economy. Producers add value. Producers take raw materials and add their labor to make them into more valuable goods. Producers offer their time and experience as services, adding value to other businesses and households. Producers are more than just purchasers or users, they are creators.

Raising producers is not the norm in our society, however. Although 82% of parents did chores when they were growing up, only 28% require them of their own children.[10] That's sad for our society and it's really sad for those children. Chores are one of the best ways to learn diligence and develop a work ethic.

Preteens and young teens are capable of far more than most people imagine—they just need some training and some opportunity. We have a rotating chore list that all the "big kids" share; when they reach the preteen years, sometimes as early as 8 years old, they get that promotion to the rotation. The major chores we expect are things like feeding the dogs and straightening up the den, doing

---

[10] Stevens, Heidi. "Why aren't we expecting our kids to do chores?" Chicago Tribune, October 13, 2014. http://www.chicagotribune.com/lifestyles/ct-kids-chores-vanishing-balancing-20141013-column.html

laundry for the family, rotating the dishwasher and washing dishes (no mean task when everyone is home!), and cooking meals. We've seen preteens in our family and others' who do things like sewing, caring for farm animals, doing yard work, even painting houses.

Once Melanie went to a Mother-Daughter Dinner and sat across from a mom and her seventeen-year-old daughter. When they heard how many children we had, they asked, "What are they doing for dinner?"

Melanie answered, "I don't know!"

The mom spurted, "What in the world do you mean? Didn't you cook for them before you left?"

"Or get them a pizza or something?" suggested the teenager.

Melanie explained that our teens would be cooking for themselves, and we left the menu to their discretion.

"Wow, I wouldn't know how to *start*," said the 17-year-old.

What in the world? A teenager who is almost old enough to leave home and doesn't know how to cook for herself has been done no favors. She's got some pretty difficult lessons to learn. Our older sons have told us, heads shaking, that they are better cooks than most of the girls they know at college.

Whether they marry young, old, or not at all, our children, male and female, will need to know how to take care of themselves. Chores prepare our children for that future and to care for their family one day. *All* our children learn to cook, do laundry, clean, and do yardwork. They need help at first—we don't want our nine-year-old carrying a pot of boiling water to the sink to drain the noodles, and a younger person may need a hand starting the leaf blower. They learn quickly, though, and they'll need a lot less help than you might imagine. Just train them what to do, emphasizing safety rules, and supervise them until they get it down. It works the same way with mowers, washing machines, or any other tool.

What about babysitting?

One of the things we look forward to as our children mature is getting their help around the house! And it is certainly useful when there are other people who can keep an eye on the littles—sometimes Mom or Dad just needs a nap!

Kids in the preteens can certainly entertain younger siblings while Mom works on something nearby. They can even supervise younger siblings doing a job, and we try to give them opportunities to be in charge for short periods. Experience taught us they generally need a parent available, though, because kids this age often struggle to control their tempers. If everyone's behaving, the young work leaders will likely be fine, but if they get any pushback, they can lose it themselves pretty quickly.

Toward the end of the preteens and in the early teen years, most properly-trained kids are perfectly able to babysit younger siblings while their parents are gone.[11] Most girls will soon be able to babysit for other families, too. We generally don't recommend that for boys due to the temptations (and possibilities of being falsely accused, too).

Adult wannabees

Kids this age really want to be grown-ups. They want to be men and women. That is a very powerful desire that you can harness to help them learn diligence!

[11] We highly recommend the Safe Sitter course taught at hospitals. It's far more safety-oriented than many courses, and it teaches children how to deal with all sorts of emergencies. You do need to check with your instructor about local regulations; some states specify how old a child needs to be before being left alone.

One of the biggest motivations you can give them is to explain how they are really contributing to the family. "Son, thank you for rotating the dishwasher. I was just talking to a mom interested in homeschooling. I was able to do that because I knew you were working hard in there and we'd be able to move right into dinner prep. That ministry was partly you. Thanks!"

They also love to have the sole responsibility for something. They want to be in charge. At this age, our kids *hated* being assigned to clean up a room with their siblings unless they were the boss. Often they didn't even want that; they wanted to do it alone! Giving them the responsibility can actually work out pretty well because they are so distractible at this age they are likely to drive anyone working with them batty! At least if the room is their job, you can immediately identify who needs to go back and try again!

Speaking of getting distracted, a common question at our house is "What are you doing to advance the family mission?" We're not talking about those huge, ambitious, century-long family missions some people talk about. Our family mission tends to be much closer in view, like "Get to Church on Time" or "Finish Cleaning before Grandma Gets Here." We want to draw our kids' attention to the fact that our family has important things to accomplish, and they need to be part of the solution, not off on their own reading or playing games. We encourage them to open their eyes to what's happening, and ask themselves, "What can I do to make it happen?" For example, they already *know* that we can't leave for church until everybody's dressed, so once they're ready, why not help the toddler with her shoes?

We often tell our children that, "Doing what you are supposed to be doing without someone forcing you" is a mark of maturity. Adults take responsibility for themselves and their jobs.

Developing a business mindset

Melanie grew up in a family business and we have the blessing of working together as a family today. Some of our young people are natural-born entrepreneurs, and we suspect several of them will be in business for themselves one day.

But even if your child is more likely to work for somebody else, it's a useful thing to have the mindset of a business owner.

We had an interesting experience one trip which gave our kids a powerful illustration. One night, we were camping in a state park, and realized at nightfall that we needed more ice for the cooler. We stepped over to the campground store, and as we approached the door, the employee stepped up on the other side and snapped the lock in our faces.

"We're closed," he said.

"We just need a bag of ice," we appealed. After all, it was still five minutes before closing time.

"We're *closed*," he reiterated, and walked away. We had to drive back into town to get the ice.

The next evening, we pulled into a rural gas station just as the lights were going off. "Oh. I guess we missed them," Hal said—when the lights suddenly came back on. With a thankful shrug, we unloaded and went inside while Hal started pumping the gas.

"So," he asked the man at the register, "are you the owner of this store?"

"Yes, I am!" said the proprietor with a smile.

When we got back in the van, we talked about the two different attitudes we'd seen and how one clerk was very willing to stay late when he saw that van with a huge gas tank pull up, while the other wasn't. Who was looking after the business? We explained that if you work as if you were the owner, with the owner's best interests at heart, you'll be far ahead of your competition.

We use this concept of developing the businessman's mindset when we talk about our children's work habits. These easily-distracted young people, just barely leaving childhood, need extra encouragement to stay on a job until it's truly finished. When they drift (or shirk), you can ask them, "If I were your customer paying you for the work you just did, would I be happy I'd hired you?"

Don't be too harsh. It's probably not a good idea to go off on a rampage, firing everyone in sight! But a thoughtful correction helps them understand that they are developing work habits that will bless or curse them in adulthood.

We also like to point out other good and bad business practices to our kids. We were driving down a remote interstate one day when we saw a billboard for a pizza restaurant that said, "Call now and pick it up hot! 30 minutes away!"

We pointed it out to our children. "What a brilliant marketing strategy!" we told them. "People pulling off at an exit to pick up some dinner usually wouldn't consider a pizza place because you have to order and then wait. This restaurant just opened up a whole new market of travelers by posting that billboard thirty minutes away from their exit!"

Practicing supporting the family

A friend of ours who was an independent building contractor lost much of his vision to an illness in his early fifties. His four teenage sons immediately stepped up to multiple part time jobs in order to keep the family bills paid while they finished high school.

That wasn't uncommon years ago, but thankfully few of our children will face that sort of challenge. However, the day will come soon enough when they will be working to support themselves and, Lord willing, a young family. You can start preparing them for that day by letting them provide for the family now, in a small age-appropriate way.

One day Melanie had a young son at the grocery store with her. He had some pocket money on him, and as usual, he began to wheedle a little, "Mom, can I buy a candy bar...or...or... a bag of candy to take home and share with the family? I've got a lot of money saved!"

Melanie started to say, "Oh, honey! Save your money! Remember that LEGO set you've wanted to buy?" She felt a little guilty that we hadn't been able to buy many things like that for the children lately, and didn't want her son to miss the item he'd been saving for.

But before the words came out, a thought popped into her head — *What would Jesus say? Would He say, "Save it for yourself!" or would He say, "Give, and it shall be given unto you!"*[12]? Oops. It was time to rethink this.

Finally, she said, "Okay. You can buy a bag of candy to share, but on the way in I saw they are having a buy one-get one free sale on ice cream today. For about the same amount of money, you could get two cartons of ice cream to share!"

"Would I get to choose the flavors?" he asked.

"Sure!" Melanie responded and they headed off to the frozen food section. You would have thought he was choosing an engagement ring, he took it so seriously! He considered what different siblings liked best and tried to figure out two flavors that would make everyone happy.

---

[12] Luke 6:38 KJV

By the time they got home, he was ready to burst. He ran in the house yelling, "Hey, I bought ice cream for a treat for everybody!" As his siblings gathered around, he set up to serve them. Later, when we were all eating, we saw him looking around and grinning at how much everyone was enjoying his treat. He was ecstatic.

We learned something that day. Our children need to learn to give. They need to learn to take joy in other people's pleasure. We resolved to stop turning them down when they wanted to buy something for us or for their siblings.

That was soon put to the test.

We used to have a Jeep which our boys drove when they were home from college. One of our sons had a minor accident which left people unhurt but the radiator cracked. It wasn't large enough for insurance to kick in, but we didn't have a repair in the budget that month either so we told the guys we'd just park it for a few weeks. A few days later, his younger brother (a new driver) came to us.

"You know that money I've been saving for a new guitar?" he asked. "Is it okay with you if I spend it on fixing the Jeep?"

Our earlier commitment was soon in tatters.

"But son, you've been saving so long for a guitar! It's so important to you!"

"I know, but I can just start saving again," he said. He had found a source for parts online and had a mechanic friend who agreed to talk him through the replacement.

Remembering the lesson we learned, we swallowed our pride (nasty stuff, pride) and okayed his plan.

A couple of weeks later, he spent the day working on the Jeep. We heard the hood bang down and our young man swaggered in. He jammed his hands in his pockets and announced, "You know what? I had no idea how *good* it felt to provide something the family really needed!"

Bingo. That's just what we were aiming for!

One day our children will be mothers and fathers making endless sacrifices for their families. What a blessing if they've learned how good it feels to take care of their family, if they've learned to take joy in the pleasure of the ones they love. The preteen years are a great time to let them start practicing that. Let your children make sacrifices for you and the family.

Real work

Often it seems we learn our kids' capabilities when circumstances force them to the front.

Our first year on the road with our ministry, Hal was diagnosed with stage IV cancer. Hal's doctor reluctantly said he might be able to keep his speaking engagements, but the chemotherapy would weaken his immune system too much for him to stand around shaking hands in the exhibit hall.

When the boys heard this, they immediately responded, "Don't worry, Dad! We'll take care of it!" And so they did. The weekend of our first conference, they jumped right into setting up the booth and working with customers. That evening, they popped into our hotel room, overjoyed, and cried, "Guess how many copies of our book we sold?" *Our* book. Not *your* book, but *our* book. We knew then that their help was going to be a really good thing for our family.

Preteens can be a huge help in the family business or ministry. Ours have thoroughly enjoyed working in our booth during conference weekends, helping assemble orders at home, and learning skills like web programming and graphic design to support the endeavor. Best of all, when kids help out in a business or ministry, it becomes their ministry, too, not just their parents'. They feel some ownership—and that greatly decreases resentment.

Melanie's family owned a chain of ladies' clothing stores, and she and her brother grew up helping with inventory and cleaning changing rooms. She freely admits that there were times she resented it. It was hard being at the store when you knew your friends were home sitting in front of the TV! Now, though, she looks back with great thankfulness. Her father died when she was only fourteen, yet because they worked side by side, talking all the while, she knew her father in a way most of her adult friends still don't.

Their own business

Preteens can work for themselves, too. Our grandparents all had businesses of their own when they were preteens and teens. They did yardwork or babysat. They delivered papers or raised doves. That became less common as the general level of prosperity grew, but we're hearing rumblings of a return to business for young people.

Carol Topp, the author of *Micro Business for Teens,* clearly points out that a student already has a job—they're a *student*—and that any sort of business opportunity has to take a back seat to that primary responsibility. Some business ideas, even if a young person has a special knack or talent for it, just don't work with school hours and homework requirements. At the most, a young entrepreneur shouldn't plan on working more than a few hours a week. But even a young preteen can run a real business part-time, if they're realistic about the time they can invest and the skills they have or need to learn.

We know one family that requires their children, as part of their schooling, to start a business at age 8, to expand it at age 10, and to start another business or open up a new line when they're 12. What does that look like? What can an eight–or ten-year-old do?

This family's daughter bought old blue jeans and belts at a thrift store. She cut the legs off the jeans and sewed up the bottoms. She sewed a belt onto each one as a handle and sold them in local gift shops as hobo bags. Her brother gathered pine cones, soaked them in paraffin wax, bundled them and sold them at local camp grounds as fire starters. Later, he started cultivating worms to sell as fishing bait, but discovered that the chickens which provided the guano the worms loved were actually more interesting than the bait business. Now he raises chickens and helps neighbors care for their coops when they're away.

We met another young teen at a conference selling handmade jewelry. A missionary speaking at her church had told how widows in his country made necklaces from beads they rolled from scrap paper. They sold these for small amounts to support their children. This young entrepreneur asked the missionary if he would be able to send her a box of necklaces and let her see if she could sell them for much higher prices in the U.S. to help support these women and their families. Now she was running a business for charity, sending all the proceeds to the missionary in Africa.

Clearly kids that young are going to need help—they can't drive for one thing!–but they can do real business. We've known other young people who made crafts and sold them online or at local craft fairs. Some have done baking or cleaning for others. Although in most places a preteen or young teen is too young to get a traditional job working outside the family, there are world of opportunities available if they're willing to strike out on their own!

Looking ahead

A s your kids move into their teens, the opportunities only get better. The traditional after-school jobs working at fast food restaurants, stocking shelves and ringing up customers at a grocery store, or doing yardwork, housework, or babysitting for neighbors, are all legitimate and honorable options—but there are all sorts of jobs they can do if we help them think outside the box.

When three of our children were 13, 15, and 17, they bought an online business from a local family, selling grain mills and small appliances on the internet. They quickly found that no one online could tell they were all teens, and customers and vendors alike would take them seriously! They learned how to deal with unreliable suppliers and angry customers. They learned how to market their products and what happens when you don't. They learned how to admit a mistake and make it right, and also how to be patient when it was the other person's mistake. They learned how to trust the Lord when it looked like several hundred dollars of merchandise had been stolen. They learned far more by doing business than they could have by just working for someone else.

One young teen we know worked as a contract janitor for a mega-church. His friends teased him, "I can't believe you clean toilets! Yuck!"

He retorted, "I can't believe you work for minimum wage!" Unusual jobs often pay more than a young adult could expect at a more typical job.

Another young man loved making films when he was a preteen and young teen. When he went to a theater, he often took a notebook with him and took furious notes about what the filmmakers got right and what they didn't. When he was seventeen, he brought his dad a movie review he'd written about a new release, asking if it was good enough to start a blog with. His dad read it and suggested instead that he might try for publication; the dad knew a local magazine editor and offered to introduce him. The editor was so impressed with the teen's work, he paid him $250 for the article and before long, the young man was doing investigative reporting for the magazine. They were very surprised to find out he hadn't even graduated from high school yet. How do you think that looked on his college resume?

One teen we knew loved gardening and began taking gardening classes at the local cooperative extension office. Before long, he'd learned enough to get his parents' weekend farm certified as an organic grower, and he quickly developed a business selling produce to local restaurants and markets.

There's really not much limit to what a teen can accomplish with a work ethic and a business mindset. Let them try!

Stewardship

Ultimately, we want to teach our children that God has given them certain gifts—financial resources, sure, but also their talents, abilities, even their family and friends—and God expects them to use all those things in a righteous way that brings Him glory.

We want our young people to learn diligence, to exercise self-control, to be wise in their use of finances. We want them to have a business mindset and entrepreneurial spirit whether they ever go into business for themselves or not. We want them to be productive stewards no matter who their earthly boss may be, because it will glorify God and make *them* more successful, too.

Most of all, we want them to view money in the right light and to place their priority on the most important things—not the accumulation of personal wealthy, but development of character and a lifestyle of service. As the apostle said, *It is required in stewards that one be found faithful...*[13]— not, he might add, that he or she necessarily be rich in the worldly sense:

> *Not that I speak in regard to need,* Paul said, *for I have learned in whatever state I am, to be content: I know how to be abased, and I know how to abound. Everywhere and in all things I have learned both to be full and to be hungry, both to abound and to suffer need. I can do all things through Christ who strengthens me.*[14]

---

[13] 1 Corinthians 4:2
[14] Philippians 4:11-13 NKJV

The Next Big Thing 12

H al was in Atlanta for a training class, and Melanie and our four small boys had come along for the trip. It was a hot day, and Melanie was wrestling our double stroller through the city zoo, the baby and the toddler in the seats, two slightly older boys hanging on either side of the handle. A passing stranger watched the perspiring young mother's exertions for a few minutes, then asked the required question—"Are they *all* yours?"

Summoning up a tired smile, Melanie said, "Yes, they are!"

"Well, if you think they're trouble now, just wait until they're teenagers!" the stranger said with a laugh.

We've often thought that was just about the bottom of our social interactions as a large family. The nadir. The end. It didn't get much more discouraging than that.

And yet we found that our kids' high school years were quite enjoyable. They were a lot of work for parent and child alike, that's undeniable. There are still things settling down after the preteen hormone flood, and there are still doubts and fears and uncertainties and weirdness that come with the time of life. We still felt like there was some growing up to do and some unfinished business yet, even when they graduated. But on the balance, we look back at the teen years now with appreciation. The stranger was a false prophet, for us.

Paul David Tripp's book on parenting teenagers is called *The Age of Opportunity*. That's what it is—a time when doors are opening and horizons beckon for these young men and women. It's the start of opportunities for them—and in a real sense, a beginning of the end of our role as day-to-day supervisors and managers. Our opportunity to guide them is going to change very soon, and we want to make the best of the years they remain in our home.

But so much of the teens' years revolve around the high school experience, our efforts at parenting are going to follow in the same orbit. Your pre-teen is about to launch; let's look at how you can prepare to be an effective counselor and coach for your young *teens*.

What track are they aiming for?

The perennial question for little children is, "What do you want to be when you grow up?" (Some of us are asking ourselves the same question in our thirties and forties.) A pop-culture proverb says that if you don't know where you're going, you're likely to end up someplace else.

In the German school system, students are grouped and sorted into tracks in middle school. Their secondary education system is much more specific than ours, with one high school leading to the university system, one directing students into the technical colleges and trade schools, and one providing a general education for future laborers.

In many ways, our school system does the same thing, without sorting the children into different campuses. Certainly, some schools are more rigorous than others, but on the whole, students track themselves within the larger system by the classes they select. There is a real difference between one English teacher and another, between one section of Algebra II and another, and between an AP History course and a purely high school-level history class.

If a student wants to make the most of the opportunities ahead, he or she needs some careful guidance on their way through high school—starting before they arrive! The aspiring engineer who ought to take calculus his senior year should really be starting algebra in the eighth grade. The student who's aiming for veterinary school needs to plan on as much chemistry and life science as she can work into her schedule. And the strategic path through these years won't come together by chance!

At this point, of course, both you and your preteen may have bulging eyes and tightness in your chests. At 13 years old, it's a very rare student who has a clear vocational calling in mind. Frankly, many good, serious students are still unsure exactly what they want to become when they reach their junior or senior years. According to the United States Department of Education, about a third of college students change their majors at least once—whether in four-year or associates degree programs.[1] Uncertainty is a common thing!

In some ways, this is built into our human existence. We can't know for certain what the future holds; we can and should plan, but with humility. *Come now,* said the apostle James, *you who say, "Today or tomorrow we will go to such and such a city, spend a year there, buy and sell, and make a profit..."* (One might say, "... go to such and such a college, spend four years there, and graduate to a lucrative job offer...") *"... you do not know what will happen tomorrow. For what is your life? It is even a vapor that appears for a little time and then vanishes away. Instead, you ought to say, "If the Lord wills, we shall live and do this or that."*[2]

God told the prophet Isaiah, *"I am God, and there is none like Me, declaring the end from the beginning..."*[3] God knows the conclusion of

[1] In some majors, like mathematics or natural sciences, the percentage approaches 50%. Reference: U.S. Department of Education *Data Point,* December 2017 NCES 2018-434, "Beginning College Students Who Change Their Majors Within 3 Years of Enrollment". https://nces.ed.gov/pubs2018/2018434.pdf, accessed 15 Mar 2018.

[2] James 4:13-15

[3] Isaiah 46:9

the matter, always; we only make our best guess, and prepare with as much wisdom and insight as we have!

That's not to sound hopeless, but rather to say, don't feel ashamed if you and your student are surrounded by question marks rather than confident assurance. Instead, make your plans based on what you *do* know! And then work with the opportunities you have.

Do you see any aptitude or attractions?

The obvious first step is to ask, "Does this young person have a history of interest in one direction?" Think generally. Has this student always had a knack for math? Has she been writing stories and poems as long as she's been able to read? Is your son a future St. Francis or Dr. Doolittle, befriending any animal he encounters?

Sometimes you have a child with a range of interests. One of ours was fascinated by laws and the Constitution, and considered whether he might aim to be an attorney someday. At the same time, he was very creative, and loved to research, write, and develop scripts and screenplays. How can you advise a broad-spectrum sort of mind like that?

Several years ago, the Gallup Organization did a massive study of American management, followed by another study of the workers they managed. One of their findings was how prone we are to cubbyhole people into convenient categories—in career terms, to say, "This one's good in math—she needs to be in the lab," or "This guy has language skills—put him in sales." Instead, they suggest, maybe we should consider the person's *whole* range of abilities and gifts, rather than zooming in on one and saying, "Specialize in this, please—and don't waste your time on the others." Too often, we fail to appreciate—and cultivate—the real personal strengths that fall outside the immediate job description.

Hal encountered two books arising from this study several years into his career, and it was liberating.[4] They gave him the freedom to recognize that yes, he was good with math and technology, but he was also a good writer and liked to work with ideas and people, not just things and numbers. The first qualities might qualify him to become an engineer (which he was at the time) but they didn't begin to explain his other interests and gifts.

Both of us went to high school at a time when anyone who could do math was strongly encouraged, really pushed, into math, science, or engineering as a major. Hal majored in Engineering and Melanie in Biology. Our true gifts, though, seem to be in writing and public speaking. Those weren't even offered to us as options.

Your child is multi-faceted, just as we were and our kids are. We explained to our son that law school and film school were very different paths, and while he wouldn't be able to pursue both at the same time, there was nothing to preclude him one day becoming an attorney who worked in intellectual property rights, or a filmmaker who not only understood the fine print in contracts but was able to use his creative gifts to make difficult ideas easy to understand. And there may be opportunities to move from one specialty to another, while still capitalizing on the gifts God had given him!

On the other hand, you may have a child who has a razor-sharp focus on one particular field—to become a doctor, to join the military, to be a stay-at-home mother, to start his own business. As an adult with experience (or one who has friends and contacts), you can help guide

---

[4] Marcus Buckingham, *First, Break All The Rules* (The Gallup Press, 1999); Buckingham and Don Clifton, *Now Discover Your Strengths* (Gallup, 2001).

that student into the academic paths that offer the best preparation for their dreams.

The one caution we offer is to leave space for God's redirection or clarification. One of our sons was always on the spot whenever there was blood; if anyone lost a tooth, broke a finger, or had any sort of medical issue, this little guy was right there and full of questions. We always thought, "This one is likely to become a doctor!" Yet later in life we realized his bent was not so much medicine as service; he is a rescuer at heart, and in a family full of boys, most of the daily heroism involved responding to mishaps! We've found he is happiest when he's able to bring his many gifts to bear to save a situation or recover an emergency—driving hours to recover a stalled vehicle, volunteering to cater a wedding or retreat, or investing overtime hours to bring a project to completion.

And some gifts have regular parallels. One of our sons was a numbers guy; even as a five-year-old, when we visited a museum to admire a great artist, he was calculating the painter's life span from the dates on descriptive cards. As he grew older, he discovered a natural gift for music—many people have discovered gifts in math and music often go to the same minds. Admittedly, we all struggled with the direction his studies should take—even the category of "musically inclined" can lead down a dozen pathways—but in the end, he embraced both gifts, studying economics in college but auditioning for the campus choral ensembles and leading worship in church.

As your kids approach graduation, it's good idea to have a brainstorming session. All of you get together and list all their talents and skills, then all their interests, and finally, all the different kinds of careers you can think of that incorporate their talents and interests. That can help them find some direction.

But no matter how your student is inclined, we found a simple rule to help us with any case. We told our children, "We don't know what God has planned for your life, so we intend to give you as broad an education as we can while you're here in our home." And that's what we've strived to do.

What do they need to know—no matter what?

Robert Fulghum had a best seller in the 1990s when he wrote, *All I Ever Needed to Know I Learned in Kindergarten.* His point was not about preschool programs—after all, so many of the milk-and-cookies pleasantries he talks about really arise first at home—as it was about manners and character which ought to be valued and universal.

From our perspective, that's a reminder that most of life is *not* guided by what you learned from textbooks. Character is important, and compassion, honesty, diligence, and courtesy are things you learn outside of class, at the dinner table and at your parents' side. But what about skills and habits which make for everyday competence in life?

One of our sons worked as a residential advisor in a freshman dormitory at college. One evening as we were talking on the phone, he abruptly ended the conversation, saying, "There's one of my man-babies—I've got to go."

On a later call, he elaborated. "I've got ninety freshmen to look after," he explained, "and frankly, they're clueless. They don't know how washing machines work, they don't know when to go to the infirmary when they're sick, and they don't know what to do about a parking ticket or a car problem. They're not adults, they're 'man-babies.'"

Whatever view you have about gender roles, equality, or complementarity between men and women, at the end of the day most kids will need to be able to take care of themselves alone, at least for a while. A major threshold to adulthood is simply living outside your parents' direction and care. Even though many young adults come back to live with their parents for a time, that ought to be a decision guided by economics and temporary circumstances—not inability to cope.

And in many areas, there's not a bright Biblical line between "men's work" and "women's work." As a practical matter, at one time there were seven males and only one Mom in our home. If Melanie wasn't going to be overwhelmed by the sheer volume of household work to be done, everyone had to pitch in. That meant that all our boys took their turn washing dishes. They learned to wash and fold laundry. They all learned to cook, too.

Likewise, our daughters need to learn to check the oil in their cars. They need to know how to change a tire. They get to run the big noisy machines that cut the grass and blow the leaves, too, even though we may tend to give the heavier tasks to their brothers—just as we might lean a little toward the girls' normal nurturing skills when supervising little ones.

Because while it's likely that most of our children will be married sometime in the future—and we need to be preparing them for that life, too—statistically speaking, there's a strong chance they'll be single for some time after they leave our homes for college or grown up life. If our kids come home from the university with a basket of dirty clothes or a car due for an oil change, it ought to be simply because Mom or Dad might be willing to do them a favor—not because they don't have the skills or the nerve to take care of themselves.

The next growth spurt

B y the time our kids reach high school age, most of them have had the big growth spurt (in height, stature, and shape). There are a few other areas to watch out for, though, and make plans to address.

There will be physical changes that continue on past high school graduation, though not as outwardly dramatic as the first ones. Many of these are connected with brain development and emotional function. We found that our fifteen - and sixteen-year-olds seemed to reach a new plateau of emotional control—much to our surprised relief.

That improvement in emotional stability comes before social maturity, though. We call it "the gormless time"—a pleasantly British word which basically means, lacking sense. They have gained the ability to reason abstractly and to come to logical conclusions, but their experience and knowledge are still limited. They make pronouncements as if they are proven fact, while adults shake their heads, "It doesn't work quite that way." They have a new confidence and poise for interacting with others, but seem to lack judgment or boundaries about what's appropriate or in good taste to bring up. They need lots of coaching at this point!

And we've got to remember that these years are the time our sons hit their intellectual stride. When they come out of the tractionless middle school years, girls tend to pick up where they slipped a few years earlier, but their brothers begin to close the gap between them and their sisters. You may be amazed at the progress they make in a very few years—the reason you don't want to set their goals in concrete based on what you see when they're 13. That's also why you need to work really hard to preserve their love of learning in the preteen years.

And over the next horizon

No one really told us what to expect when our little ones were still little. Other than half-joking, half-dire warnings about the awfulness of teenagers, we didn't hear anything about the years between kindergarten and... *then.*

So, we wanted to share some of the things we learned... when we got over the shock. And admittedly, we didn't really start to understand them until our third or fourth child. You may not have enough children to learn it the same way... and besides, we wish someone had told us before our *first* child hit this weird and wonderful transition.

When we wrote our first book about parenting sons, we called it *Raising Real Men*—because we find the longer view is what we have in mind. We're aiming for adult men, not older boys. The title of this book was chosen along the same lines. We're not hoping for successful teenagers, but well-prepared adults; they were little before, but no longer—ever!

So how have ours turned out?

We certainly have to give all the glory to God, not to our wisdom and superior parenting techniques. He is the one who made them—and us—temperamentally what we all are. There are no guarantees in parenting, and even that most hopeful of verses—Proverbs 22:6, *Train up a child in the way he should go, and when he is old he will not depart from it*—only tells us that our early training will impact the rest of their lives... even if they depart for a time, in the meanwhile.

But we will say this: though our grown sons are all different in personalities and gifts, they have all continued in the faith we taught them, even when we could no longer compel them. They've walked different pathways through high school and college, and their careers are very different, but they've moved forward into the early years of independent adulthood with courage and persistence.

And we've enjoyed a friendship that grew between us as they matured. They'll always be "our kids," and yet we have fellowship with them now as believers and fellow adults. We enjoy their company. They ask our opinion and listen to our advice whether they invited it or not—but then they make their own decision, with prayer and consideration. We even ask for their advice and prayer support on a regular basis. Our adult kids have become our best friends.

They have been through some shocks. While some were in high school, they had to deal with their father's bout with cancer and a baby sister's treatment for a congenital heart defect. They've had setbacks in job aspirations or relationships. They've had car trouble and financial stress and some personal injuries, too. But we've seen them grow through the struggles and come out on the other side with stronger faith, stronger character, and practical experience from the journey.

And none have felt they had to throw off their parents' and family's teaching, or embrace a lifestyle of revolution and rebellion, or put emotional and physical separation between themselves and their family, in order to make their own decisions or chart their own course. We've all learned when to disagree and how to do it with grace. As parents we've successfully transitioned from "benevolent dictators" to "trusted advisors," where our role is to coach, not command. And surprisingly enough, it seems the guidance and nurturing we poured into them at an early stage still shapes their decisions as adults—perhaps even better than if we had tried to control and direct them as grownups.

All in all, we have to say—with thanks to God—they're pretty amazing adults. And we trust that with His grace, the same can be true of *your* preteens someday. There's hope! And it's coming sooner than you think.

So, protect your relationship with your tweens. Keep teaching them truth in that context—a loving, healthy, communicating relationship. And trust God for the results.

References

Amazing Grace. Directed by Michael Apted. (Los Angeles: Walden Media, 2006)

Barnier, Carol. *Engaging Today's Prodigal: Clear Thinking, New Approaches, and Reasons for HOPE.* (Chicago: Moody Publishers, 2012)

Bauer, Susan Wise. "What Is Classical Education?" *The Well-Trained Mind*. Peace Hill Press, n.d. Web. 31 Mar 2016. http://www.welltrainedmind.com/classical-education/.

Blakemore, Sarah-Jayne, Stephanie Burnett, and Ronald E. Dahl. "The Role of Puberty in the Developing Adolescent Brain." *Human Brain Mapping* 31.6 (2010): 926-33. *PubMed Central*. Web. 10 Aug 2015.

Buckingham, Marcus. *First, Break All The Rules* (Washington, DC: Gallup Press, 1999);

Buckingham, Marcus and Don Clifton. *Now Discover Your Strengths* (Washington, DC: Gallup Press, 2001).

Business Insider. "'Fifty Shades of Grey' started out as 'Twilight' fan fiction before becoming an international phenomenon." *Business Insider*, 17 Feb 2015. http://www.businessinsider.com/fifty-shades-of-grey-started-out-as-twilight-fan-fiction-2015-2 Accessed 31 Mar 2018

Challies, Tim. "Counterfeit Detection (Part 1)." Challies.com: Informing the Reforming, 27 Jun 2006 <http://www.challies.com/articles/counterfeit-detection-part-1> Accessed 3 Apr 2016

Covenant Eyes, Inc. *Porn Stats: 250+ Facts, Quotes, and Statistics About Pornography Use.* (Owosso, MI: Covenant Eyes, 2015). http://setfreesummit.staging.wpengine.com/wp-content/uploads/2016/01/2015-porn-stats-covenant-eyes.pdf. Accessed 3 Apr 2016

Franklin, Benjamin to Madame Brillon: Letter and Printed Bagatelle ("The Whistle"), 10 November 1779," *Founders Online,* National Archives, last modified July 12, 2016, http://founders.archives.gov/documents/Franklin/01-31-02-0041. [Original source: *The Papers of Benjamin Franklin, vol. 31, November 1, 1779, through February 29, 1780,* ed. Barbara B. Oberg. New Haven and London: Yale University Press, 1995, pp. 69-77.]

Forster, Pam. *For Instruction In Righteousness A Topical Reference Guide for Biblical Child-Training* (Oregon City, OR: Doorposts, 2011)

Gundersen, Dennis. *Your Child's Profession of Faith.* Updated edition. (Sand Springs, OK: Grace and Truth Books, 2010)

Ham, Ken. *Evolution: The Lie.* Revised and expanded edition. (Green Forest, AR: Master Books, 2012)

Ham, Ken and Britt Beemer with Todd Hillard. *Already Gone: Why your kids will quit church and what you can do to stop it* (Green Forest, AR: Master Books, 2009)

Henry, Matthew. *Commentary on the Whole Bible* (6 vol.). Original publication 1708-1710.

Lewis, C.S. *Mere Christianity*. Original publication 1954. Reprint edition. (San Francisco: HarperOne, 2015).

Madigan S, Ly A, Rash CL, Van Ouytsel J, Temple JR. "Prevalence of Multiple Forms of Sexting Behavior Among Youth: A Systematic Review and Meta-analysis." *JAMA Pediatr*. Published online February 26, 2018. doi:10.1001/jamapediatrics.2017.5314

McDowell, Josh. *Evidence That Demands a Verdict*. (San Bernadino, CA: Here's Life Publishers, 1986)

McKie, Robin. "Onset of Puberty in Girls Has Fallen by Five Years since 1920." *The Guardian*, 20 Oct 2012. http://www.theguardian.com/society/2012/oct/21/puberty-adolescence-childhood-onset. Accessed 3 Apr 2016

O'Toole, Jennifer Cook. *The Asperkid's (Secret) Book of Social Rules: The Handbook of Not-So-Obvious Social Guidelines for Tweens and Teens with Asperger's Syndrome*. (Philadelphia: Jessica Kingsley Publishers, 2012)

Ray, Brian D. *Gen2 Survey: A spiritual and educational survey on Christian millennials* (Salem, OR: National Home Education Research Institute, 2015). Overview available at https://www.nheri.org/gen2-survey-a-spiritual-and-educational-survey-on-christian-millennials/. Comments taken from personal notes at Gen2 Leadership Conference, January 30-31, 2015.

Stevens, Heidi. "Why aren't we expecting our kids to do chores?" Chicago Tribune, October 13, 2014. http://www.chicagotribune.com/lifestyles/ct-kids-chores-vanishing-balancing-20141013-column.html

Strobel, Lee. *The Case for Christ: A Journalist's Personal Investigation of the Evidence for Jesus*. (Grand Rapids, MI: Zondervan, 1998)

Swift, Jonathan. "On Poetry: A Rhapsody" (1733). http://www.online-literature.com/swift/3515/. Accessed 30 Mar 2018.

The Federal Reserve System. *The Federal Reserve Payments Study 2016*, December 2016. https://www.federalreserve.gov/newsevents/press/other/2016-payments-study-20161222.pdf. Accessed March 4, 2018.

U.S. Department of Education *Data Point*, December 2017 NCES 2018-434, "Beginning College Students Who Change Their Majors Within 3 Years of Enrollment". https://nces.ed.gov/pubs2018/2018434.pdf. Accessed 15 Mar 2018.

Weil, Elizabeth. "Puberty Before Age 10: A New 'Normal'?" *The New York Times Magazine*, 30 Mar 2012. Web. 12 Aug 2015.

Young, Hal and Melanie. *Love, Honor, and Virtue: Gaining or Regaining a Biblical Attitude Toward Sexuality*. (Smithfield, N.C.: Great Waters Press, 2017)

Scripture Referenced

Genesis

1:28	59
1:31	60
2:18ff	126
24	86
39:6	153

Exodus

20:12	123

Leviticus

19:14	79

Numbers

1:3	130
4:3	130

Deuteronomy

5:16	123
10:14	152
32:35	99

1 Samuel

16:7	22
17:33	129
17:42	129

1 Kings

12:1-16	130

2 Chronicles

13:7	130

Psalms

34:14	116
50:10	152
127	108
127:4	129

Proverbs

5:18	128
14:1	116
14:9	98
17:17	117
18:22	89
19:11	76, 120
22:6	184
22:7	158
25:28	24

Isaiah

5:20	98
46:9	177
55:11	124

Index

Colophon

This book is set in 14-point Neuton, a strong serif face designed by Brian Zick and inspired in parts by the Dutch Old Style tradition. It lends stability and matter-of-fact readability to long-form body paragraphs.

The accompanying display face is Josefin Sans in a variety of weights, an elegant, modern geometric sans on vintage lines penned by Santiago Orozco. Occasional details from the humanist tradition likely trace back to similar influences on classic 1920s geometric sans such as Kabel.

Sister typeface Josefin Slab by Santiago Orozco is used on the cover. Economica Bold, designed by Vicente Lamónaca, is additionally used for chapter numbers. Interior layout and typesetting performed in Adobe InDesign CC by John Calvin Young.

45370923R00117

Made in the USA
Columbia, SC
21 December 2018